The University Library
UNIVERSITY OF CALIFORNIA / RIVERSIDE
D1010955

Go See the Movie in Your Head

94

Go See The Movie in Your Head

Joseph E. Shorr, Ph.D.

ROSS-ERIKSON PUBLISHERS, INC. SANTA BARBARA

The first edition of this work was published in September, 1977 by Popular Library, a division of CBS Inc.

Second Edition, September, 1983
ISBN 0-915520-65-6

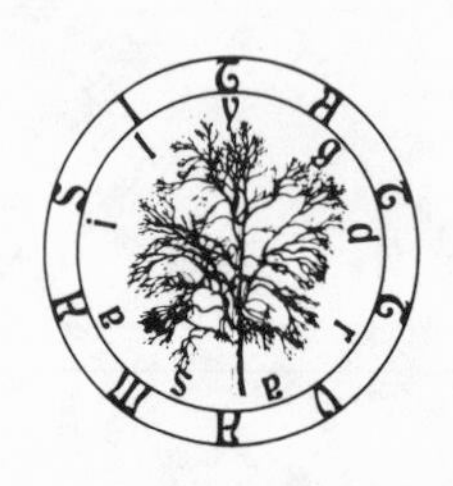

Ross-Erikson Publishers, Inc.
629 State Street, Santa Barbara, CA 93101

Composed, printed, and bound in the United States of America
1 2 3 4 5 6 7 8 9 10

Contents

Acknowledgments

It is impossible to name everyone who helped me and encouraged me to write this book.

I deeply appreciate all of my patients for their imagery, from which I have learned so much about the power of human imagination.

I am grateful to all the persons who enrolled in my classes in "Imagery and Human Growth" at UCLA. I learned much from them. I learned equally from the many professional psychologists and counselors who attended my ten- and twenty-week training classes as well as those who attended the various seminars and workshops in imagery.

I want to thank each member of the staff of the Institute for Psycho-Imagination Therapy for support and suggestions: Jack A. Connella, Michelle

Lawrence, Marilynn Lovell, Pennee Robin, Gail Sobel, and Dr. David Tansey.

A word of thanks to Drs. Virel, Fretigny, and Boucher, who gave me the privilege of presenting my work to the International Congress of Mental Imagery in Paris in the summer of 1976.

A special acknowledgment must go to the pioneering work of Dr. Jerome L. Singer of Yale University for his encouragement in the exploration of imagery approaches in psychotherapy.

Much appreciation is due to Pennee Robin for her tireless, loving help in editing and reorganizing the manuscript. Her assistance was invaluable.

Finally, I want to express my thanks to Charlotte Gordon of Popular Library for her excellent suggestions and editorial assistance.

Foreword

Neither Columbus nor Marco Polo ever saw more fascinating sights than you will see when you involve yourself in this book. You, too, have a new world to discover—your inner world of imagery.

Previously unrevealed vistas of the imagination can now be explored through a concise, intensive, and systematic investigation of your waking imagery. All you need to embark on your journey is the willingness to trust the images that come to you.

Thousands of pictures flow through your mind in the course of a day. The waking imagery of each person is unique. Now it can be captured and comprehended with a new and original approach. I have spent the past twelve years developing Psycho-Imagination Therapy. This fruitful method can now be used readily by nearly everyone.

You are the stage manager, producer, director, and subject of your own waking imagery. The meaning of your images, of necessity, relates back to your own life experiences. As you read this book you will learn how to use your imagery to become aware of how you see the world and to recognize the strategies you have developed to steer your way through a tricky physical and social environment.

I have found that imagery is the key to the inner world of the individual. Through imagery we glimpse the world as others see it. We also learn to see our own world with different eyes as we learn to interpret our images.

Perhaps the most important aspect of imagery as I use it is its ability to bypass the usual censorship of the person. Very often, when you express your thoughts verbally, you edit them. You may not want others to know what you really feel. You may even be hiding things from yourself. When you are asked to imagine a specific situation, you do not usually know in advance what it will reveal. Imagery has the capacity to break through the resistances employed in verbal transactions.

The systematic analysis of your mental panorama can lead to greater self-awareness, increased sensuality, and creative solutions to your problems. Tuning in to your imagery can reveal to you your internal conflicts and increase your capacity to change them effectively. You learn how to reveal yourself to yourself, and you will understand better how others see you.

As you explore the fantastic world of imagery

you see the extent to which it colors and guides your life. Dual Imagery helps you get in touch with your most basic conflicts. Self-Imagery reveals your feelings about yourself and your self-concept. Body Imagery clarifies the way you really sense your body and what your body feelings mean.

Spontaneous Imagery, Parental Imagery, and Task Imagery throw light on your world view, your attitudes about life, your guilts and fears, how you relate to others, and how you think others feel about you.

Sexual Imagery gives you insight into your true feelings about your own sexuality and sensuality and your attitudes toward the opposite sex. It should free you for greater enjoyment and intimacy.

You will learn to focus for change through Task Imagery and Cathartic Imagery. The images in your dreams are also opened for your inspection and you are shown how to use them productively.

"Go see the movie in your head" and you will find a way to know yourself; you will learn to recognize what you want to change and how to do it; and you will have an exciting technique for catching a glimpse into your own inner world. Worth the price of admission!

Joseph E. Shorr, Ph.D.
Los Angeles, California, 1976

PREFACE TO THE SECOND EDITION

IN THE SIX years since *Go See the Movie in Your Head* was first published, interest in the field of imagery has grown by quantum leaps. Imagery, which for over a half century was not considered a fit subject for study, is now a full-fledged movement. Scholars throughout the country are exploring the nature of mental imagery, and its various aspects are now the basis of some doctoral dissertations. On the international level, scholars and clinicians are sharing information in conferences and publications.

I no longer feel as alone as I did in 1970 when I gave what I believe was the first university course in mental imagery at UCLA. Since then, I have given classes and workshops in mental imagery and Psycho-Imagination Therapy in Sweden, Austria, Germany, England, France, and Japan, as well as at several universities in the United States.

In 1979, I founded and became the first president of the American Association for the Study of Mental Imagery. The cross-fertilization of ideas and the sharing of experiences, both in research and in clinical application, resulting from the annual conferences and the publishing of the proceedings have created a climate wherein several journals devoted to the nature and clinical use of mental imagery in medicine, psychotherapy, and self-improvement are now produced regularly.

The main body of the book has been left unchanged because the theoretical stance upon which Psycho-Imagination Therapy is developed is unchanged. Although written for the general public, this book covers all the salient points covered in my first two books which were written for professionals. (A second edition of those books has just been released in a single volume.) The major additions to my theory and application of imagery are the expanded categories of imagery and additional empirical validation of the diagnostic value and therapeutic interventions of Psycho-Imagination Therapy.

In the years since the first edition of this book, I have explored in depth the categories of body imagery, sexual imagery, parental imagery, self-image therapy, and group therapy imagery and have written articles about each. I have edited and helped with the preparation of several volumes of the proceedings of the American Association for the Study of Mental Imagery and have contributed articles and chapters to books by other authors. All of these will be found in the expanded bibliography at the end of this volume.

Work has also been progressing at the Institute for Psycho-Imagination Therapy on projective tests using imagery. We have published the Shorr Imagery Test and the Group Shorr Imagery Test and are preparing for publication the Shorr Parent Child Imagery Test, and the Shorr Couples Imagery Test. These tests all use Imaginary Situations and Sentence Completions to reveal hidden conflicts and patterns of interaction.

I want to correct one error made in the first edition. In Chapter Three, I cited an article from Perceptual and Motor Skills on "Hypnotizability, Laterality of Eye Movements, and Brain Asymmetry." This article was written by Dr. Paul Bakan (not Dr. David Bakan) of Simon Fraser University of Vancouver, B.C., who is now president-elect of AASMI.

In Chapter One, there is a list of sentences to be finished. I have since added two more to the list. These have proved to reveal a great deal more about the subjective meaning of Imaginary Situations. I suggest that you include them when you are exploring your own imageries for additional depth of understanding. They are:

I fear ________.

Never refer to me as ________.

Ensuing work with the "Three Doors" Imaginary Situation in Chapter Six has been found to reveal another level of information. The middle door has consistantly continued to reveal aspects of sex and intimate relationships. The left and right doors clearly spell out a conflict in one of the doors, and the possible resolution in the other. There is no clear-cut pattern as to whether the conflict will appear behind the left or the right door. However, if you enter into the image and explore it, become the image and finish the sentences as if you were the image, you will come to know behind which door you perceive the conflict and can expect some clue to the resolution behind the other, which you also enter and explore in depth.

Waking imagery has the quality analogous to dreams as both are avenues into the person's unconscious. When persons report the flow of their waking imagery, they are revealing dimensions of personality of which they would not ordinarily be aware. Waking imagery, thus, has a projective quality that bypasses most ordinary censorship. This function of the mind is often neglected in verbal linear interaction with the therapist. Images flowing through our heads are instantaneous, effortless, and ubiquitous; they are taken for granted. The images flowing through our heads in one hour of life may reveal countless meanings about ourselves. The "discovery" of waking imagery, its uncovering qualities combined with the ability to find meaning in its productions, may be one of the more important psychological findings in this century; and the one most ignored. Our waking images are often so fleeting that no method should be spared in capturing them and then finding meaning in them.

My thanks to Dr. Jerome L. Singer of Yale University; Dr. Eric Klinger of the University of Minnesota; Dr. Bengt Göran Fasth of Gotteborg, Sweden; Dr. Milton Wolpin of the University of Southern California; Dr. Paul Bakan of Simon Fraser University; Dr. David Tansey of San Diego; and Dr. Erma Dosamentes-Alperson of the University of Southern California for their gratifying support and encouragement as well as for their contributions to the study of mental imagery and their role in keeping AASMI viable.

Special thanks and acknowledgement go to Dr. Jack Connella, Pennee Robin, and Gail Sobel-Whittington, the loyal and hard-working staff of the Institute for Psycho-Imagination Therapy for their contributions to the use of mental imagery in psychotherapy as well as their efforts to establish norms and prepare the manuscripts for the various Shorr Imagery Tests.

They have used Psycho-Imagination Therapy in their private practies at the Shorr Clinic, they have given workshops for laymen and professionals, and they have helped with the day-to-day mechanics of maintaining the Institute for Psycho-Imagination Therapy and the Shorr Clinic.

I am especially appreciative of the painstaking editorial work and organization of the original manuscript of this book done by Pennee Robin, and I thank her for continuing that job in order to bring to life this second edition.

Joseph E. Shorr, Ph.D.
Los Angeles, 1983

CHAPTER I

The Fantastic World of Imagery

There is a movie constantly running in your head. Images flow through your mind in an ever-changing, never-ceasing stream. Yet you are often unaware of the existence of these pictures until you are involved in an intense daydream, are suddenly startled by a nightmare, or find an unbidden image intruding into your consciousness.

You may say you never have images. This is extremely unlikely. Vivid or hazy, we all have them. Jerome L. Singer of Yale, in his book *Daydreams*, says his studies show that 96 per cent of the population reported daydreaming. There are images in our heads constantly, regardless of what kind of thinking, reasoning, problem-solving, or wishing is going on. Since we are all image-making and information-processing persons, why not let our images work for us?

In this book you will be asked to experience images while you are reading. I will start by asking you to perform a simple exercise that may open a whole new world to you. This is the kind of Imaginary Situation that I often give my patients in Psycho-Imagination Therapy. All you have to do is to be sure you are comfortably seated; sit back, relax, and let the movie inside your head unfold before you. Trust your flow of imagery—it will open the door to your "private theater."

> Imagine walking up to a fence. There is a ladder leaning against it. Climb the ladder and look over the fence. What do you see? What do you do? What do you feel?

Were you able to imagine this sequence? Did it surprise you? Did it have any meaning for you? Sometimes when people do this exercise in imagery they see what is going on in their lives at the present time. Other people see things in the future. For some it indicates a life barrier that must be crossed over.

You may want to jot down your image or record it on an audio cassette so that you can return to it later when you have learned more about the meaning of your imagery and how to use it. Be sure to include your feelings as you experienced the image. I will go into greater detail in interpreting this image later.

If you had trouble doing that imagery sequence, you probably just need a little help and encouragement to get you started. It is possible that you image a lot without actually being aware of doing so. For instance, think of what happens when you give someone directions to come to your home for the first time. You probably start with an image of where the person is coming from. Then you form a mental map of how to travel the distance between the two points. It is from this mental map that you give instructions about where to turn right or left and provide the landmarks which make the trip easier. You do the same thing when you are in a hurry to get from one place to another. You mentally run through alternate routes so that you can select the one which presents the least delays and obstacles.

In the charming movie *Hester Street*, the landlady, speaking to the hero, says: "You can't pee on my back and make me think it's rain!" In order to comprehend, you probably visualized such words as "pee," "on my back," and "rain." It was your image-making ability that made you understand. As you can see, communication between people depends a great deal on image making.

Do you need more proof? Try this: Image telephoning a person you have never met. As you hear the voice, do you get a mental picture of what the person looks like? Can you image the surroundings? Most of us do this without even being aware that we are doing it. Then we meet the person and we are startled to find that he or she is—or is not—as we pictured.

Let's go back to that movie in your head. Most of the time it is a montage of fleeting images. Occasionally, as in a daydream, there is a full script with characters playing out a drama. You rehearse how you will ask your boss for a raise and then imagine his response. Perhaps you relive the quarrel you had with your spouse last night and then rewrite the scene adding all the "I should have said . . ."s.

Both sight and sound images occur in our heads. Our image-making capacity is what makes watching a movie or television, reading a book, or listening to the radio so enjoyable. It is also what makes it possible for the creator to write the book, the movie, or the radio script. Every artist, no matter what his medium, relies on imagery. He translates his images into something that the rest of us can experience. Entertainers perform their own or someone else's images and make them real for us. In sharing our images, we communicate.

We are all familiar with visual humor. The Marx Brothers, Charlie Chaplin, W. C. Fields, Laurel and Hardy, and numerous other comedians inspired laughter by their clothes, their make-up, their pantomime, and the ridiculous situations they created.

There is also a vast repertoire of humor that stems from imagined scenes of what we hear. The stand-up comics could not perform if it were not for the audience's capacity to conjure up images. Shelly Berman creates the scene of driving a car and dropping the lit end of his cigarette in his lap. As a busload of people watch him, he tries frantically to put out the fire without having his movements construed as sexual. We do not have to see him in person. Just hearing his record is enough to make us see the humorous images, innuendoes, and implications.

Radio depends on images for its very existence. If we didn't have an image of Fibber McGee's noisy, cluttered closet, we would have no awareness of the humor. Jack Benny, Charlie McCarthy, and George Burns and Gracie Allen created whole worlds of hilarious images for us.

Radio imagery, of course, is not limited to humor. Fantasy, terror, and mystery lend themselves equally well to imagery. Orson Welles's famous broadcast describing a Martian attack on Earth was an outstanding success. People imagined it to be the real thing. I doubt if seeing the same drama on television could have had such a stunning impact. Welles succeeded far beyond his expectations.

The eerie notes of The Whistler or the sinister voice of The Shadow, signaling their approach, were sufficient to send chills of fear racing along listeners' spines. The recent revival of "CBS Radio Mystery Theater" testifies to our interest in terror imagery.

Just as we make images out of what we hear, we certainly do so when reading. The printed words on the page create images of travel, adventure, mystery, humor, and fear. We translate the words into pictures and live what we read.

At times we use our imagination to transform the ordinary into an adventure, thus preventing boredom. Take for example Washington Irving's story, "The Stout Gentleman."

Irving's central character, forced to spend some time in a gloomy and uninteresting country inn, idly generates an intriguing story to occupy himself. Overhearing several references to a "stout gentleman" who occupies an upstairs room in the inn, the character imagines what the stout gentleman must be like. Circumstances encourage the character to envision him as unyieldingly aristocratic and openly lascivious. In the end, as the stout gentleman actually boards a carriage, the storyteller gets only a glimpse of the man's expansive posterior. In essence, the story involves the narrator's ability to turn the tedium of the inn into a mildly exciting and speculative adventure. Almost all of us at some time have concocted stories to forestall boredom.

Perhaps the greatest master of literary imagery was Franz Kafka. So vivid were his images, his name has become an adjective: "kafkaesque." Here is an image-provoking excerpt from the opening paragraph in his short story "The Metamorphosis":

> As Gregor Samsa awoke one morning from uneasy dreams, he found himself transformed in his bed into a gigantic insect. He was lying on his hard, as it were armour-plated, back, and when he lifted his head a little he could see his dome-like brown belly divided into stiff arched segments on top of which the bed quilt could hardly keep in position and was about to slide off completely. His numerous legs, which were pitifully thin compared to the rest of his bulk, waved hopelessly before his eyes.

Recurrent image patterns—sometimes referred to as leitmotifs—are common in theatrical plays and in the opera. These related metaphors are a unifying agency. They occur also in poetry where the function of imagery is highly varied: imagery foreshadows events, lends atmosphere to particular occasions, helps to differentiate speakers and to underscore themes. Images are the vehicle by which the poet's thoughts reach the reader's imagination.

Imagery exercises the imagination in two

ways: first, by making us see things; second, by making us interpret what we see. Many writers and readers say that characters "come alive" precisely because their images become clear and in motion. George Bernard Shaw said that once he imagined his characters, they took over and acted the play for him. Imagery in action released his creativity.

Dante's *Divine Comedy* is the best-known Italian literary work in America. Actively competing for second place are *The Decameron* by Boccaccio and *Pinocchio*, a little book for children, written by an otherwise obscure author named Collodi.

It is understandable that *The Decameron* should have such popularity because of its universal themes, but it is truly amazing that *Pinocchio* should be so well-known. What is so fascinating about the story of a wooden puppet?

Unlike his siblings, Pinocchio did not need a puppeteer to move his strings. He was capable of motions on his own. From the moment that Geppetto, the carpenter, gave the last touches to his legs, Pinocchio "came alive." He kicked his "father."

Pinocchio was not happy as a wooden puppet. He wanted to be a real boy. As the story evolves he becomes tamed, socialized, industrious, and acquires a conscience. When this gradual transformation is completed, he has miraculously changed into a child of flesh and blood, a regular member of the human race.

First, we have been captivated by the image of a puppet who can move by himself—who behaves as if he were alive. Then we begin to identify with his transformation from puppet to human. Just as Pinocchio has achieved his goal, so too can we transform ourselves into the persons we want to be.

Most of us, when we use our creative imaginations, are initially stirred by some alluring puzzle which calls for a solution. We are enabled by our own creations in the mind to see much that before was dark or unintelligible. As our images take coherent shape we see more clearly what has puzzled and perplexed us.

Let's return to your imagery exercise of the "fence and ladder" as an illustration of how imagery helps us see things and then interpret them. My words evoked an image in your head. But the words "fence" and "ladder" can induce different pictures for different people, based on their understanding of the words and their past experiences. Furthermore, asking what you saw, did, and felt were open-ended questions that tapped into your unique life position. The words lead to pictures with basic similarities but with the possibility of near infinite variety. So, just as we seek meaning in literary imagery, we also can seek meaning in our own imagery.

I suggested that the "fence and ladder" imagery exercise could represent something going on in your life right now, something you see in the future, or it could focus on an obstacle facing you. Think carefully about what you saw, felt, and did in the image. Do you begin to get an inkling of all that was contained in that image?

To help you further with interpretation, here is how one of my patients responded to that imaginary situation. Keep in mind that no two responses are alike. The first time he climbed the ladder and looked over the fence, he saw orderly rows of trees. This was not in line with his previous open approach to imagery. It suggested to me some resistance to facing difficult things in himself. Some time later I had him repeat the same imaginary situation. The second time he saw snakes, monsters, and eyes staring at him. He was terrified. I urged him to cross over the fence, and when he did he was amazed to see the snakes and monsters running away from him. The eyes turned into his terrible father who also ran away from him. He was suddenly overcome by a feeling of peace. His imagery helped us both to see what was going on within him, and through it we were able to interpret and cope with hidden material.

In make-believe play, the child is literally manipulating or acting out images. We often see children engaged in conversations with imaginary companions, or with real companions who are not present at the moment. Living imagery in children has been described as the third dimension of their personality.

This dimension is equally important to adults. The couple in Albee's play, *Who's Afraid of Virginia Woolf?*, sustain their relationship by creating an imaginary twenty-one-year-old son. When the husband finally reveals the nonexistence of the son, the fiction of their relationship is revealed. Such fictions are necessary for certain relationships. Imagination has creative and positive value to enhance relationships also. Frank Barron writes, "The sorcery and charm of imagination, and the power it gives to the individual to transform his world into a new world order and delight, make it one of the most treasured of all human capacities."

But what exactly is the nature of this capacity? Where do our images come from? How do they fit into the general scheme of mental functions? What makes them so special that we devote a book to them?

Up until now we have been examining the creative aspects of imagery. Let's take a look at its origins and at its basic nature. In her book, *Spearpoint*, Sylvia Ashton-Warner beautifully describes the organic origin of imagery in man:

> Organic work is not new but as old as man; as old as that first animal-man who stood erect from apehood. His grunts were not for nothing, they meant some want or fear; guttural utterances which were the captions to the pictures in his hairy mind, symbols of the images of what he needed for self-preservation and for social preservation.
>
> Survival imagery first . . . water and food; imagery of what he feared . . . enemy, thunder, famine. Then radical imagery . . . woman, children. The urgency of his feelings about these needs forced the pictures from his mind into his throat and out upon his tongue to communicate them to another.

Certain environmental images have always been part of man's life. The original function of the environmental image is as an aid to finding one's way. A correct mental map can mean life or death to a primitive tribe. The Luritcha of central Australia, driven from their territory by four years of drought, survived by the precise topographic memory of the oldest men. These elders, using experience gained years before, together with the instructions of their grandfathers, knew the chain of tiny water holes that led them across the desert to safety.

The terror of being lost comes from the necessity of a mobile organism to be oriented to its surroundings. Have you ever wondered where your car was parked when you attended some crowded event and then tried to locate the car by the image of where you had parked it? Instead of water holes, you were using a modern version of wayfinding to locate a parked car.

The organic need for orientation to the surroundings may be the basis of powerful emotional associations. The search for life-giving water holes can generate terror or panic. The search for a parked car will probably evoke only annoyance or momentary anxiety, but modern man faces situations as terrifying and as dangerous as those experienced by primitives. Put yourself in the place of the naval aviator who becomes disoriented while flying.

> *. . . take off and rendezvous were normal. Captain M. made frequent rapid turning movements of his head from side to side to see that his flight was intact. Vertigo suddenly developed. He had a feeling that his plane was peeling off in a steep left-hand dive, and had a strong desire to use right rudder and right aileron, but saw by his instruments that he was flying straight and level. "It took all the guts I had to believe those instru-

* Witkin, *Orientation in Space* (*Research Reviews* for Office of Naval Research, December 1949).

ments," he said, "but I knew they were right and that my sensations were wrong."

> . . . Captain M. stated that no combat experience had frightened him as had this attack of vertigo. He felt helpless and had a cold fear of impending doom. He had a strong tendency to tighten up and freeze at the controls.

Imagery can also serve an adaptive function by helping us reorient old patterns of behavior to changed situations. Roger M. Downs and David Stea, in *Image and Environment*, tell of a woman who:

> . . . once applied imagery to help her master left-hand driving before touring England and Scotland. In flight and just before falling asleep, she saw herself in a car designed for left-hand drive. She drove the roads, imagining she was coming out of a one-way street, entering into complicated turns or traffic patterns. "And," she added with a grin, "the system really works."

Imagery is valuable, not only in the sense in which it acts as a map, but in a broader sense it can serve as a general frame of reference within which the individual can act or to which he can attach his knowledge. Storytelling among nonliterate people depends on images of past events. In this sense it is like a body of beliefs or a set of social customs; it is an organizer of facts and possibilities.

Walter Lippmann, the former dean of journalistic evaluation of political and social phenomena, early in his career proceeded on the assumption that concepts were directly related to, and even dependent on, mental imagery. He wrote in *A Preface to Politics*:

> The only feeling that anyone can have about an event he does not experience is the feeling aroused by his mental image of that event. . . . No idea is lucid for practical decisions until it has visual or tactile value. . . . what each man does is based not on direct and certain knowledge but on the pictures made by himself or given to him.

Lippmann's words point to a key concept in the nature of imagery. The influence of past experience is vital in the organization and production of visual imagery. We may reorganize or transform our images, yet nothing develops from nothing. We must have some past experience as a basis for our imagination. Perception, or the ability to see and absorb what is seen in the world of sensations and social interaction, must precede the ability to make images and to reshape them.

There are various means of creating images from sensory experiences. Lacking sight, the blind rely on hearing, smelling, touching, and action for stimulation. Very often they transform images from one sense to another. A blind man, George, under the influence of auditory melodies, re-creates the visual images of the Morse code which he first encountered in a physics course he took while he could still see. Another blind man, Nathaniel, under the same influence, re-created visual images of printed letters.

The re-creation of images in adult blind persons can occur with a limited reliance on immediate sensory elements. In Skorokhodova's book *How I*

Perceive and Picture the World Around Me, the blind Russian woman includes a section called "How I Picture What is Occurring on the Stage." In describing the national dance of a Cossack she notes:

> He seemed to be of medium size (although I was not told what size he was), with a laughing face and quick, sure movements. I could not visualize the upper part of the costume, but there seemed to be wide sleeves which billowed out during the dance; I visualized the lower part of the costume as wide bell-bottom trousers. As a result of sensing the sounds of the music (a piano) and the pounding of feet, I could visualize how fast and with what enthusiasm the Cossack was dancing. His "fire" dance infected me; I was so electrified that I was ready to swear that I saw the dancer, that I was feeling his blouse with the billowing sleeves and his face inflamed with the dance which seemed to smile, showing strong, well-formed teeth. The image of the dancing artist arose in my imagination only because I sensed the vibrations of the gay music and the feel of the brisk footfalls.

The creative imagination is obviously a powerful means of reconstructing complex visual-kinetic, audiovisual, and other types of images.

Although the eyes have been called the windows of the soul, they are not so much peepholes as entry ports, supplying raw material. The eye and the brain do not act as a camera or a recording instrument. Neither in perceiving or remembering is there an enduring copy of the optical input. Visual memory differs from perception because it is based primarily on stored, rather than on current, information. When we recognize someone we haven't seen for a long time, we perform the act of recognition by correlating the person in front of us with the memory previously sensed of that person, which we have recorded in the form of a mental image.

There is another aspect of visual memory which differentiates it from perception. As an illustration I suggest that you try to recall your earliest memory. Did you see yourself in that image? When you had the experience as a child, you were not able to view yourself; but in your recollection, you were able to construct a picture of yourself (as a child) to fit into that scene.

UFO's are also constructions. At present we have no way of knowing for certain whether they are real or not. The Air Force investigations have disproved about 85 per cent of the sightings so far reported. But what about the other 15 per cent? Whatever they are finally proved to be, they are still real images existing in our minds.

Imagery is a common human characteristic—almost everyone has the ability to image. Now I want to go a step further and show that imagery is predominantly a human characteristic. It has been demonstrated that rudimentary images do occur in some animals. However, imagery is basic to one of the uniquely human attributes—the ability to symbolize. If we use "symbol" to mean something which stands for something else which is not present, the image must be considered one of the first symbols. The most common example is language. All words are symbols. "Food" is a symbol for the things we eat. "Water" is a symbol for the combination of hydrogen and oxygen that falls as rain or flows through the pipes of our houses. "Page" is a symbol for this piece of printed paper you are reading.

If several people are all talking about a person who is not present but who is known as Martha, they all may have an image of Martha in their minds, and an agreement can be reached by all that the word "Martha" is a symbol of the person Martha. An interpersonal process has taken place as a result of which the word has taken the place of the person. Thus verbal symbolization requires an interpersonal relationship and as such helps us exchange experiences.

There is a further dimension in symbolizing. You can close your eyes and visualize someone—your mother, for instance—who is not present. But her image is with you; it stands for her. The image is obviously based on the memory traces of previous perceptions of your mother. She then acquires a psychic reality which is not tied to her physical presence. Usually the image of one's mother is also a synthesis of what one thinks, feels, and knows about her.

The image thus becomes a substitute for the external object. It is actually an *inner* object. If emotional associations are pleasant, it reinforces our longing for that external object. The image then motivates us to search out the actual object. After all, the actual object is still more gratifying than the image.

The opposite is also true. If our image associations are unpleasant, we do not want to exchange the unpleasant inner image for the unpleasant external object.

Social scientists agree that the infant is not born

with the ability to tell the difference between an imagined event and one that has actually occurred. How does the baby learn to make the necessary discrimination?

First we know that when an event occurs, the person knows what is happening because he looks, he hears, he smells; his knowledge is derived from sensory impressions. Such messages seem to be registered in the nervous system so that, during recall, the images and sensations can be re-experienced although less vividly. It is commonly assumed that everyone is born with this capacity to recapitulate events. K. Koffka, the Gestalt psychologist, suggested that a "trace" is left in the infant which permits a partial re-experiencing of the event at a later time.

Given this assumption, we may postulate that once an infant has been hungry and then fed, the next time he becomes hungry he should have images of being fed. Since he has no inborn concepts about reality or fantasy, he cannot distinguish between his memory and the true occurrence. Nobody knows how he finally learns to tell them apart.

Babies seem to begin experiencing images sometime around the seventh month. For instance, if the child is able to look for a rattle when the rattle has been hidden under a pillow, presumably the image of the rattle can be carried in the mind. Babies' fascination with the game of peekaboo may reflect their pleasure in making the first discriminations between the two kinds of perceptual experience.

Hunger may delay the discrimination between the two kinds of imagery or cause the child to replace the image of a real bottle by a fantasied one.

When images appear in our mind's eye, as in dreams or waking imagery, we must make some "image hypothesis" to give it a coherency and meaning. Have you ever seen a stream of images in a movie that seems to be unconnected and random? If you have, you were probably annoyed and wanted to turn away because it made no sense. We can become confused or even fearful when we cannot make sense of images. In short, we are continuously trying to find meaning in our awareness. Without the inner perception of our images in some systematic order, meaning cannot exist.

This is especially true of the way we imagine events in advance of their occurrence. This can be called reality testing. For example, as one approaches a red light in an emergency dash to the hospital, various alternatives flash through the mind. On the one hand, one envisages a traffic summons, an accident to another car, an injury to a pedestrian. On the other hand, he sees a chance of saving a precious second (and therefore a life). Imagery, therefore, has a valuable function in normal living, for it provides a method by which alternatives can be tested without undergoing all the dangers involved. This relates to what is known as forethought, foresight, anticipation, plan, purpose, and goal.

It is important at this point to make a distinction between spontaneous imagery and directed imagery. The most common form of imagery is spontaneous and arises before our inner eyes: without apparent stimulus from any specific source. The late psychologist, Augusta Jellinek, originator of the term "spontaneous imagery," stated in an article in *American Journal of Psy-*

chotherapy, in 1949, "These images are experiences as they would originate independently as if we were only spectators and not the source of these productions."

Directed imagery is the type that follows the suggestion that you imagine certain situations. An example is the one at the beginning of the chapter when you were to imagine the fence and the ladder. Directed imagery has the advantage of channeling the flow of images and giving us greater access to their meaning. But the responsibility for the imagery flow is still the individual's no matter where the suggestion comes from.

The following exercise will introduce you to spontaneous imagery:

> Picture five consecutive images. Write them down. Examine the five images to see if they seem to form some pattern. Were you surprised by any of them? Which one had the strongest feeling as you imagined it? Does some meaning in the imagery come to the forefront?

The chances are high that you can get even sharper meaning if you take the exercise one step further. You are to imagine that you *are* the image sequence that you had the strongest reaction to, and then speaking as if *you are that image*, finish the sentences:

I feel ________________.
The adjective that best describes me is ______.
I wish ________________.
I must ________________.
I secretly ______________.
I need ________________.
I will ________________.

My experience with imagery used in this way indicates that you are probably getting at something within your own experience that has a great deal of meaning to you. You may be confirming something you already know, or even more likely, you are uncovering something about yourself of which you were not aware.

It is often useful to combine words and images to crystallize meaning. Words elicit images and images elicit words. Try some imagery-related words and see what you discover. After reading each word in the following list, close your eyes and try to associate an image with it.

The Words	The Images
love	
apples	
God	
old people	
a teacher	
the beach	
London	
mother	
lion	

Probably you had the strongest reaction to one image. If so, what meaning does it have for you?

Look over all your images and see if there is some pattern to your response. You may recall some early experience or reveal some current concern.

Another exercise in imagination is to write down the next five words that spontaneously occur to you. They can be any words at all.

After you have written them down, you are to imagine an image for each word.

Now choose the image that had the strongest reaction in you and then imagine that *you are that image.*

Speaking *as that image*, finish the following sentences:

I feel ______________________________.
The adjective that best describes me is ________.
I wish ______________________________.
I must ______________________________.
I secretly ___________________________.
I need ______________________________.
I will ______________________________.

What do these answers say about you? Give it some thought.

Although it may seem that our imagination is limitless, all of us do have some built-in limits. The average person can exercise some control over daydreams, and other forms of waking imagery, but has little control over his dreams. Rarely does a person forget his daydreams, yet nocturnal dreams are often difficult to recall and frequently only snatches of a dream can be recaptured.

Each of us has different ranges of experience which serve as natural limitations to our imagination. For example, if a Chinese farmer were to imagine someone eating, he would probably imagine him using chopsticks rather than a knife and fork.

Even if we let our waking imagery flow unrestrained and free, we still have some limits, some controls. People who redo a directed imagery a month or so after the first experience often will allow to emerge what they could not the first time. This is especially true as they make changes in their openness or if they resolve certain conflicts.

I remember one young man who had great difficulty even imagining his face when asked to imagine seeing himself in a variety of situations. One day, he was finally able to see his own face. He was so moved that he cried. His inability to see himself stemmed essentially from shame and self-hatred which prevented him from seeing himself. In therapy he worked through some past shameful experiences and then was able to face himself. The changing waking imagery followed his own changing allowability.

There are images that are so strong initially they are preserved for a long time; sometimes they last for months or years, often for an entire lifetime. Most visual images seem to make a quick, strong impression. In a study conducted a few years ago, the subjects were given 2,560 pictures and allowed to examine each for only seven seconds. They were then given a packet containing the original pictures mixed with 2,560 unfamiliar pictures and asked to select the ones they had seen. They were able to identify 98 per cent of the pictures.

Ernest Kris, in *Psychoanalytic Explorations in Art*, helps explain some of the power and endurance of imagery:

> We know from clinical experience that visual images do, in fact, play a different part in our mind from that played by words. The visual

> images have deeper roots, are more primitive. The dream translates the word into images, and in heightened states of emotion the image may impose itself upon the mind as hallucinatory perception. No wonder that the belief in the special power of the visual image is particularly deep-rooted. Image magic is one of the most ubiquitous forms of magical practice. . . . The lover who tears up the photograph of his faithless love, the revolutionary who pulls down the statue of the ruler, the angry crowd burning a straw dummy of a hostile leader—all testify to the fact that this belief in the magic power of the image can always regain its power whenever our ego loses some part of its controlling function.

You are the source of your own imageries. They come from your perceptions and reflect your own personal emotional associations with them. They are a private record belonging only to you, yet it can seem you are the spectator and not the source of your images.

It is a truly remarkable sight to see people surprised by their own imagery. Sometimes their faces smile or show anger. It makes some cry, others laugh, and still others anxious.

Ordinarily, when a person is asked a question about himself, he offers a verbal reply which has been subjected to some internal censorship. He may monitor his response out of a conscious fear of disclosure. Imagery bypasses that censorship. A person does not usually know in advance what his imagery might disclose and as a result is not guarded. Through speech processes we can deny something negative about ourselves, or by clever verbal maneuvers or rationalizations we can project another point of view, but it is difficult to disavow that we have "seen" a monster in our guts.

But we are not stuck with the monster. Images can be transformed into something wholly new and are often the basis of personality change.

Imagery and self-concept are closely intertwined. We all have a self-image—"How I see myself." Sometimes it may be as an idealized image and at other times as a despised image. These are images that we can transform. If we do not want to think of ourselves as weak, we can change an imaged kitten into a tiger.

We are also concerned with "How I see you" or what image I have of you. This may be further complicated by other imagery such as "How I see you seeing me" and, further, "How I see you seeing me seeing you."

I have asked patients to imagine themselves as Humphrey Bogart imagining how Bette Davis would act if she were Groucho Marx. Funny? Complicated? Yes. Yet, that is what is going on all the time in all of us as we interact with others.

Portia Nelson has written a poem which shows this point beautifully·

> He loves me for who he thinks I am
> but,
> who he thinks I am
> is not who I am.
> Therefore,
> it's hard for me to be who I am
> when we're together,
> because I think I have to be
> who he thinks I am.

Of course, I don't know exactly
who it is he thinks I am.
I just know it isn't who I am.
Who am I?
Well . . .
Who I am is something I recognize
when someone tells me
who I am not.
At least, I think that's not who I am.
Maybe who I am not
is who I am.
If that's who I am . . .
My Gawd! He really loves me!

There is an American Indian proverb which says that one person cannot understand another without walking a mile wearing the other's moccasins. You can't really know me until you can see the world through my eyes and vice versa. But how do we get inside each other's heads to see the other's world?

How does the world look to a man or woman who is sad, furious, happy, aggressive, sexual, guilty, conscience-stricken, loved, fat, ugly, etc? And how does the world look to a man or woman at home, at work, on vacation, in a sexual situation, alone, with members of the same sex, in school, in crisis, in war, with nature, with people close to him, etc.?

In short, how does man view his "lived" world? Phenomenology aims at describing the experience of the individual in a situation. This viewpoint holds that man is best comprehended in the light of that which is unique to him and in reference to his concrete situations in the actual world. To be understood existentially, one must be considered as existing now in a certain way, although constantly engaged in becoming something different as the result of one's past, present, and future.

Imagery is the simplest way I know to understand the phenomenology of another person. A reported image is a person's unique expression of a particular phenomenon. We will both have different images for a given word or situation. But when we report them to one another, we begin to see the world through each other's eyes. This can help us become aware of the other's motivations, desires, fears, and needs.

Can our imagery motivate us? It is an inescapable fact that a motivated person or organism knows what it is after, whether or not its object is within its field of vision. A patient who imagines his hands to be dirty actually washes them. A person who, hallucinating by the use of drugs, thinks he can fly actually attempts to do so. So-called normal people may pursue pipe dreams for entire lifetimes. Advertisers have a thorough comprehension of the motive power of imagery; they know that although a product may not conform to the image they have constructed for it, the image itself is potent enough to keep the product selling. Madison Avenue hucksters conduct surveys of purchasers' desires, thoughts, and what they imagine they want; then the objects to be sold are advertised in line with an image of what the consumer desires.

You may be aware of how advertisers motivate us constantly with imagery. What may surprise you is that the Behaviorist School of psychology in the twenties and thirties, under the leadership of J. B. Watson, said there was no such thing as imagery. Watson referred to it as the "fiction of imagery." In place of imagery, he developed the concept of subvocal speech: the thought must be uttered silently before the habitual act arises. There is no evidence for "mental existence" or "mental processes" of any kind according to Watson. The role of imagery was driven out. The Behaviorists denied it life.

A series of unrelated factors which did not fit into the Behaviorists' model of the mind led psychologists back to the study of imagery after long neglect. Occurrences of hallucinations in people who were obviously not mentally disturbed; the growth of interest in psychopharmacology, especially drugs like LSD; and new studies in sensory deprivation all contributed to the turnabout in thinking. It became apparent that pictures in the mind would have to be considered and examined in order to explain these phenomena.

Imagine you are engaged in a monotonous, repetitive, unchanging task. Are you becoming drowsy? Are you beginning to daydream?

Imagine you are trapped somewhere and have not eaten for two days. You have water but no food. What kind of fantasies do you have?

Imagine you are in solitary confinement in a prison. You have food, water, light, but no one to talk to. You have no books, no radio, no television, nothing to write with or on. How will you pass the time?

We know from experience that the longer people are exposed to stimulus-deprived conditions, the more intrusive and intense their imagery becomes. Many examples of stimulus deprivation come to mind: deep-sea diving; lone survival at sea, in the desert, or in polar regions; solitary imprisonment. There has been a series of firsthand accounts of persons who have been imprisoned in concentration camps and interrogated by the police of totalitarian regimes. Studies of people deprived of food have shown that there is a marked increase in daydreams about eating. The Plains Indians knew this centuries ago. Warriors used to go out alone into secluded spots and deprive themselves of food and water to bring on dreams or hallucinations—visions—that would reveal their totem animals or their guiding spirits.

Numerous situations which require long spans of time devoted to monotonous, repetitive tasks frequently result in a form of hallucinating. Truck drivers on long-distance night runs alone have visions of cars that are not there, or of "jack rabbits big enough to step over their trucks." Other drivers on long straight roads experience "highway hypnosis." Jet pilots flying straight and level at high altitudes, radar operators monitoring a scope for a long time, operators of snowcats and other polar vehicles in intense snowstorms have all been troubled at times by the emergence into consciousness of vivid imagery, mostly visual but sometimes kinesthetic or auditory, which may momentarily be taken as reality.

Studies are just beginning to scratch the surface of the nature of imagery. Gradually we are becoming more and more aware of the impact that imagery has upon our lives, of how images develop, and how they function.

An ancient scholastic axiom states, "*Fortis*

imaginatio generat causum." (A strong imagination begets the event itself.) Historically, nothing was as motivating as man's image of paradise. Images of paradise allowed the Christians to approach the lions in the Colosseum without apparent fear.

The Laplanders used to worship large stones of eccentric shape. Not today. God is worshiped as a solid only by so-called backward people. The concept of God evokes a different mental image for each individual. Indeed when we imagine God, we impute to Him the power to have imagined us and by an act of Will to have created us.

By our imagination we can make new universes which are in line with our heart's desire. The image of a worthwhile world, of a "scheme of things in which I can be of use" appears frequently in our private fantasies. We often have a conception—sometimes recurring in dreams, or as a dim memory image—of some wonderful world in which at some time, in some way we will lead a happy existence. The conception is nebulous, but associations suggest that it refers to the unknown world of healthy living. In spite of its vagueness, this image exercises a dynamic pull. It may serve only to reinforce neurotic attitudes, since we feel reluctant to commit ourselves fully to anything in the present and perhaps forfeit some future opportunity for this unknown happiness. Sometimes the good world is imagined to be in some distant place. This notion, reinforced by the relief we often feel when away from the tasks and relationships of daily life, gives rise to the frequently encountered dreams of travel. A patient who was planning a stay in Europe said: "Italy stood for paradise; in going there I would wipe the slate clean, drop my phony ways, and lead a genuine life."

Images can be as important and powerful and, in some cases, more important than external reality. The individual uses imagery not only to understand the world better, but also sometimes to create a surrogate for it.

The next seven chapters will show you how to understand and interpret your images, how to use imagery to change your own self-definition and how others define you, how to recognize and resolve inner conflicts, how to understand and enhance your sex life, and how to create the kind of person you want to be in the world you want to live in.

CHAPTER II

The Images that Give Meaning to Your Life

If you sit in a relaxed manner with your eyes closed, you are very likely to have mental pictures. Of course if you wish to "see" certain things, those are what you will probably visualize. Sometimes mental pictures occur while you are doing something else, or when your eyes are open and staring off at one point. These waking images can also be referred to as daydreams. I prefer "waking imagery" as the term to describe these images because daydreaming has been more closely allied to wish fulfillment. Waking imagery is a more all-inclusive term.

In waking imagery, unlike night dreams, we are aware of the imagery processes, and we can also engage in dialogue with our images. Experiencing the imagery with emotions, sensations, and thoughts is a common human situation. Most of us have vivid memories of what we have experienced during a sequence of imagery.

As children we imagined monsters in shadows and trembled with fear when our fantasies transformed strange sounds into something menacing. Now as adults we are not so often alarmed by our images because we have learned to select between inner and outer reality. But there are times when we react to our images as we did in childhood.

Imagery is a picture of anything that goes on in your mind. It sometimes approximates a movie sequence. At other times it is a series of fleeting and seemingly unconnected pictures. However it occurs, it is going on constantly. For instance, when you write something down on your marketing list, you are using your imagination to think of needing, say, some oranges, and you are probably picturing an image of oranges when you think of them. Or when you make a note on your desk calendar about a business appointment, you are using your imagination to understand that a meeting is going to take place and an image of the other people's faces may enter your mind. Or perhaps you picture a meeting room with people around the table. Imagery goes on in our heads all the time. If you think about it, you will notice it happening.

Another way that imagery—imagination—sometimes works is to frighten us or to make us happy about something that's going to happen later today or next week—something that we can imagine but that has not yet happened. Or it may be something that has happened in the past that we cannot get out of our minds.

Remember, not all your images will be camera

sharp and perfect. Often your images may be soft and somewhat fuzzy. Of course, we do know how clear some images can be, but even if they are not perfectly clear, our images are an important part of our inner world. Sometimes a fleeting image instantaneously experienced can be as meaningful as the most sharply perceived image.

There are also those images that intrude into our consciousness and stay for a time sequence that we find disconcerting. These unbidden images stay despite our desire to have them disappear. It has been suggested that these intrusive images are akin to obsessional thoughts.

I think all of us have had images that keep coming into our heads after we have felt foolish about something. We may re-experience the situation over and over. When we are in love, there are images that keep entering our minds and we find they keep coming "in." In the musical *South Pacific*, the heroine tries to "wash that man right out of my hair."

Not all unbidden images are negative, however, for there are positive images that return and return without the need for us to press some magic button. A persistent daydream of a wish-fulfilling nature may repeatedly penetrate our consciousness as well. But in general, there seems to be more of a continuous imagery flow in a timeless fashion, unpredictably entering and leaving without apparent reason.

If we could accurately recapture a single hour's sequence of imagery flow and put it on film, as it were, with a corresponding sound track, we would still be faced with an enormous task of understanding what, why, how, who, and where. But primarily "Why *that* image?" and "Why the next?" and so on would lead to a labyrinth of interconnections and patterns that may defy ordinary investigation.

It is, however, possible to view your images systematically and to find meaning to them. I have spent the past twelve years developing a theory and technique for using imagery to reveal the private personal world of my patients and to help them solve life problems. This book will show you how to do the same thing for yourself, using your waking imagery.

In the first chapter you started doing imagery. Now I am going to teach you how to explore and interpret your imagery. Examining your own unique image production can be a route to self-knowledge.

Your imagery and questions should tell you:

1. How you define yourself in relation to others.
2. How you feel others define you.
3. The kinds of conflicts involved.
4. If you are ready to face conflicts.
5. Resolving conflicts with the aid of imagery.

Let's try another imagery exercise right now. Remember to sit back, relax, close your eyes, and let the imagery flow.

> Imagine you are a walnut. What do you see? What do you do? What do you feel?

If you are like most people, you understand a bit of what your imagery was saying to you. If you didn't seem to get anything out of it, don't think this technique won't work for you. It will. No image is really insignificant, although some images have more meaning than others, and sometimes we need help in ferreting out the meaning.

How did you feel as the walnut? Did you get a feeling of being closed in? Or were you feeling safe within the shell? This image could be telling you that you feel threatened by the outside world and want to be insulated from it. It could, on the other hand, suggest that you are feeling trapped by life circumstances and you want to break out. As you can see, when you explore your unique reactions to this image, you begin to get some perspective on what is happening inside of you. As you examine and interpret your responses to the other imaginary situations in this book, your insights will develop and you will see patterns of feeling and behavior that may have been hidden before. You will perhaps become aware of your defenses as well.

The importance of imagery as a key to your inner world is not something new. Freud, Carl Jung, Sándor Ferenczi, and others worked extensively with imagery techniques. But for the greater part of this century, under the influence of J. B. Watson and the Behaviorists, who primarily emphasized conditioning, those who dealt with the mind and its mysteries actually denied the existence of imagery. (Although the psychoanalysts kept the interest in imagery alive through exploration of dream-imagery, it is only during the past two decades, after a fifty-year lapse, that psychologists have again begun to investigate the phenomena of imagery in human life.)

It may seem strange that a tool so valuable

would be denied. The Behaviorists did not want to deal with phenomena they could not quantify, measure, and control. Freud, on the other hand, had different reasons for eventually turning his attention elsewhere. As far back as the early 1890s he was using imagery techniques, to discover feelings and self-images that he had been unable to bring to light with hypnotism.

Freud called the process his "concentration technique." He would press his hand firmly on the patient's forehead, explaining that while he pressed, the patient would see pictures of his life. He was to communicate to Freud whatever the picture or idea might be, holding back nothing even if it seemed undesirable or frightening. Freud was enthusiastic about this technique not only because of the information he was able to interpret from the images, but also because the patient could understand much of it, could recognize that the symbolism came from his own depths, and that it truly represented him. Freud described his results in *Studies in Hysteria*, written with Joseph Breuer:

> . . . I decided to proceed on the supposition that my patients knew everything that was of any pathogenic significance, and that all that was necessary was to force them to impart it. Whenever I reached a point where to my question, "Since when have you had this symptom?" or "Where does it come from?", I received the answer, "I really don't know this," I proceeded as follows: I placed my hand on the patient's forehead or took her head between my hands and said, "Through the pressure of my hands it will come to your mind, the moment that I stop the

> pressure you will see something before you, or something will flash through your mind which you must note, it is that which we are seeking. Well, what have you seen or what came into your mind?"
>
> On applying this method for the first time . . . I was surprised to find just what I wanted, and I may say that it has since hardly ever failed me; it always showed me how to proceed in my investigations and enabled me to do all such analyses without somnambulism.

Freud later abandoned imagery for the techniques of free association because of problems of resistance and transference which he felt developed because of the physical closeness of the concentration technique. If he had continued his work with imagery, working through whatever problems he found with it, he might have continued to discover his patients' basic feelings and concepts in more depth and more rapidly than through verbal methods. As Jerome L. Singer states in *Imagery and Daydream Techniques Employed in Psychotherapy*:

> . . . Freud may have erred in not insisting on imagery alone rather than allowing patients to shift to free verbal association. He might have gotten more powerful . . . uncovering more rapidly from his earlier technique. Undoubtedly individual practitioners have sensed the importance of fostering greater emphasis on concrete imagery by patients and have found themselves impatient with the apparent glibness or defensiveness that often characterizes verbal free association.

Carl G. Jung, throughout his life, investigated the most subtle recesses of imagination. On December 12, 1913, he began his own self-analysis, resorting to the technique of provoking the upsurge of unconscious imagery and its overflowing into consciousness. He recorded his dreams daily; he also wrote down stories. He imagined himself digging into the earth and into underground galleries and caves where he encountered many kinds of strange figures. Then, according to Henri F. Ellenberger in *The Discovery of the Unconscious*, "... he had to examine carefully each image from the unconscious and to translate it, insofar as this was possible, into the language of consciousness." On his eightieth birthday, Jung stated that those early images and the lessons learned from them always remained with him and were beneficial.

Over half a century ago, Sándor Ferenczi, the most innovative of the Freudians, asked his patients to "fabricate" a fantasy or imagine one, that is, tell "... all that comes into their mind without regard for objective reality." He sometimes offered fantasies which he felt the patients *should* have been experiencing until the process took over within them.

Ferenczi claimed in *The Theory and Technique of Psychoanalysis* that his "forced fantasies" had an unquestionable analytical value because they brought about the production or reproduction of scenes quite unexpected by either patient or analyst, "... which leave an indelible impression on the mind of the patient" that aided perceptibly in advancing the analytical work. They were important also because "... they furnish a proof that the patient is, generally speaking, capable of such psychical production of which he thought himself free, so that they give us a grasp of deeper research into the unconscious."

In more modern times, Erich Fromm, Roberto Assagioli, and Jerome L. Singer, as well as many other psychologists, have explored and advocated the use of imagination in eliciting feelings and meanings.

Psycho-Imagination Therapy moves on into a myriad of new dimensions. It is a systematic way of using more than a dozen categories of imageries in depth for personality analysis and understanding. Moreover, it emphasizes imagination as the central kernel of human consciousness combined with a self-and-other personality theory. This theory is often referred to as Phenomenology.

The phenomenologists, most notably R. D. Laing, seek to understand man's view of himself as symbolized in his images. It was Laing's book, *The Self and Others*, that helped me to organize my own beliefs about self-identity and conflicts within ourselves when one part of the self-image is in conflict with another part or another person. This concept is basic to everything that will go on in this book, and I will constantly refer to it.

You have certain images about yourself, what kind of person you are. This is what we call your self-image or self-concept or self-identity. It is extremely important since it affects everything you think of and plan for yourself. Imagery explorations can help you to get in touch with how you really feel about yourself. This is the first step in deciding what things, if any, you would like to change.

A slip of the tongue, according to Freud, is a

slip of the verbal report. But how many slips of fleeting images have you had? If these were examined, they might uncover hidden thoughts and feelings more quickly. Your automatic censor may screen out words, but imagery can, and usually does, bypass the censor before we can disallow it.

Your own imagery is one of your most private possessions. You are the producer, stage manager, and director of your own imagery. Nobody else can have your images. They are unique representations of your inner world and how you see and experience it.

Learning to image your goals can help you achieve them because the imagining is like a rehearsal in advance of the real thing. Some people believe that creatively imagining makes you more open to opportunities when they arise and makes you receptive to ideas that can lead you where you want to go.

Were you surprised when you did the imagery exercise a few moments ago? Surprised that you could picture yourself as a walnut? Some people feel inhibited about letting their images out at first, but it soon becomes very easy to do. Did you have any *feelings* about what was going on in the imagery? Many people do have emotions about it even the first time they do it. Those feelings are important: they are some of the clues that help you interpret what your imagery means. Imagination has a fascinating mysterious quality to it. To discover those mysteries within yourself is extremely exciting and rewarding, particularly if you have always thought of yourself as a dull person without much spark and imagination. You can discover a part of yourself you may have always longed for when you release your own internal imagery. The magic is part of you and is yours to keep forever.

Do another imagery sequence now for deeper insight.

> Imagine looking through a magnifying glass. What do you see? What do you do? What do you feel?

This imagery sequence often uncovers hidden material. Did you discover something heretofore unrevealed? Perhaps you focused on some current concern. Or you may have brought up something from the past which you could not allow yourself to be aware of.

You may ask how your image could reveal such deep thoughts and emotions. Your images are yours. They are from your storehouse of knowledge and experience. They are often symbolic and they require examination and interpretation. Try to understand what the symbols in the image mean to *you.*

Here is what one person reported for that image:

> I looked through the magnifying glass at the names in a telephone book. Before, the type was blurred and my eyes ached from trying to focus. I needed to find the name and number and I felt frustrated. When I looked through the glass, the print was sharp and clear and I found exactly what I wanted. I felt a sense of relief from the ache in my eyes, and I was grateful because I had the number I needed and could make an important call.

I asked her what name she was seeking, but she did not know. She did not feel the name itself was so important, but rather that she could see clearly. She remarked that she was thinking of the old cliché about the phone book being printed in smaller type every year. When I inquired whether she was concerned about growing old, she replied, "That is not bothering me unduly right now. I think the image was telling me that if I examine things more carefully, or in a different way, I will be able to see more clearly. That seems to fit with some of the things I am wrestling with in my life right now."

Obviously, what you see in your imagery will have meaning specifically for you. You will find with practice that it becomes increasingly easy to discover what your imagery is telling you.

I must point out now that the word "meaning" is used in different ways throughout the book. When you search for *"meaning" in your images*, you are looking for the relationships between the symbols and pictures and your life situation, your thoughts, your feelings, and your behavior. You will examine your images and see what they can tell you about yourself that you may have been repressing.

When we talk about *"meaning" in life*, we are referring to purposes and to goals. We all reach out for meaning. Life does not seem to make much sense unless we can see a purpose to it. As Rollo May said, in an article in the *Review of Existential Psychology and Psychiatry*, ". . . you can live without a father who accepts you, but you cannot live without a world that makes sense to you."

Bruno Bettelheim has pointed out that hope for

the future sustains us in the unavoidable adversities we encounter throughout life. But hope for the future, and meaning, are not something we suddenly acquire with chronological maturity. We learn bit by bit who we are, what we are, what we want to do, and how to cope with life's dilemmas. Throughout the gradual development in childhood, we learn to distinguish the rational from the irrational, to clarify our emotions, to recognize anxieties and aspirations, to search for solutions to problems, and to develop self-confidence. Much of this is done in the imagination, by spinning daydreams and rearranging elements of fantasies and fairy tales into new situations.

Edith Weisskopf-Joelson reported in an article in *The Annals of the New York Academy of Sciences* that in a detailed study of the autobiographies of five hundred college undergraduates she found about thirty per cent of them felt they were living "lives devoid of meaning." Some felt their lives lacked meaning in the sense that they had no purpose or goal. Others claimed that their lives seemed meaningless because they lacked explanations and interpretations with regard to themselves in the world in which they lived. A third group said thoughts, wishes, and daydreams were not related to external reality and that they were disinterested in the world around them. All lacked the creativity to mix fantasy and reality in a way that would provide meaning in their lives. Tangentially, Weisskopf-Joelson states, "People tend to focus on meaning more often when they feel it is absent than when they feel it is present."

Imagination is a person's way of organizing reality and finding meaning. We remember the past and can relate it to the present and future. In this book we will be working with the past, present, and future, and you will see clearly how imagination provides structure and meaning to our lives.

Most of us experience a sense of meaninglessness at a time of loss, or at a time of failure in something important to us. This, and our feelings of grief or hopelessness, can become so strong that we cannot imagine any reason for going on. Nothing we are doing really "means" anything to us—getting up in the morning, going to work or looking for a job, meeting with people, even eating. Life loses its meaning after loss, or when the future is obscured, or we feel doomed.

In his novel *The Roots of Heaven*, Romain Gary tells the story of French prisoners in a German concentration camp who used their imagery to restore morale.

> In a German concentration camp during the war, the French prisoners are becoming increasingly demoralized; they are on a down staircase. A man called Robert devises a way to arrest the decline. He suggests that they imagine an invisible girl in the billet. If one of them swears or farts, he must bow and apologize to the "girl"; when they undress they must hang up a blanket so she can't see them. Oddly enough, this absurd game works; they enter into the spirit of the thing and morale suddenly rises. The Germans become suspicious of the men and by eavesdropping, they find out about the invisible girl. The Commandant fancies himself a psychologist. He goes along to the billet with two guards, and tells the men: "I know you have a girl in here. That is forbidden. Tomorrow I shall come here with

these guards and you will hand her over to me. She will be taken to the local brothel for German officers." When he has gone, the men are dismayed; they know if they "hand her over," they won't be able to recreate her. The next day the Commandant appears with his two soldiers. Robert, as the spokesman, says "We have decided not to hand her over." The Commandant knows he is beaten; nothing he can do can force them to hand her over. Robert is arrested and placed in solitary confinement. They all think they have seen the last of him, but weeks later he reappears, very thin and worn. He explains that he has found the way to resist solitary confinement—their game with the invisible girl has taught him that the imagination is the power to reach out to other realities, realities not physically present. He has kept himself from breaking down by imagining great herds of elephants trampling over endless plains....

For many of us, life in modern society lacks essence and meaning. It is for this reason that many people, particularly youngsters during the past decade, have gone out into the country to live off the land and to rediscover "the meaning of life." They believe that struggling for survival, instead of having everything they need furnished for them, will help awaken them to the joys of living. Goals have meaning, whether it is the goal of maintaining sanity in a prison camp or the need to prepare food and fuel against the coming winter.

Striving toward a goal gives us a sense of purpose, a feeling that we mean something to ourselves and others, whether our goal is religious, or to love and feel loved.

In therapy sessions I sometimes ask a patient to finish the sentence:

My whole life is based on proving that———.

or

My whole life is based on denying that———.

Finish either of these sentences. In the answer you will catch a glimpse of the goal, meaning, and direction that now structure your life.

For most of us, having dry, monotonous work, in which there is little responsibility and no variety of choices, fosters a sense of meaninglessness and takes away from the flavor of life. We do not feel necessary.

Inventing a purpose for a meaningless job will not solve the problem in the same way that inventing the woman gave meaning to the men in the prison camp. For the prisoners had a real goal—their survival and sanity. In a meaningless job, as in a meaningless life, making up a goal would also be meaningless and empty. What your mind is capable of doing, however, is to visualize a real goal from your own desires that will give true meaning to your life. When you start on this kind of path, your life begins to have meaning again. Perhaps you already have goals toward which you work, and perhaps you can learn to pursue them more realistically and creatively. Perhaps you can dare higher goals. In our pursuit of goals, however, we must never forget to take pleasure in living today.

Some people are frightened at the idea of making changes in their lives, even good ones. Others are frightened at the thought of changing jobs, though their job may be causing them severe emotional pain because of its uselessness or because it leads away from everything the person desires.

Some people cannot believe that they are capable of making changes that would make them happy. One excuse is that they are "too old to change." What this means is that they are *afraid* to change. They may be afraid of failing, or they may be so used to their old, accustomed selves that they cannot imagine being any other way. They are afraid to lose their old identity for fear of not having an identity at all.

What I am trying to say, simply, is that we all must have meaning or die, and that imagery—the ability to imagine—helps make meaning possible. It is a sustaining (and creative) force.

In addition to greater meaning in your life, I am attempting to teach a systematic way of using imagery to become aware of your conflicts and a way of doing something about resolving them.

You may want to work on imagery with someone close to you. Later I will give you imaginary situations to do with a significant other person in your life that will clarify and strengthen your relationship. But this is not intended as a social activity to be done for entertainment. Interpretation of images is subtle and serious—even if sometimes your images make you burst out laughing and fill you with joy.

CHAPTER III

The Tug of War Within You

"To be, or not to be . . ." With those words Shakespeare had Hamlet pose the ultimate conflict—whether to live or to die. Conflict in some form is as natural as breathing, although it is seldom a life or death matter. Surely you have suffered the indecision of choosing between two equally compelling alternatives many times.

Perhaps you were trying to decide whether or not to get married. Or whether to get a divorce. Perhaps you were choosing between continuing school and getting a job. Maybe it was as simple a choice as deciding what to wear on an important occasion. Each situation, whatever its ultimate importance, was a moment of conflict.

Maybe right now you are caught in one of those situations and you can't choose between them. There is a kind of imagery that can expose your conflicts and even help you resolve them. I call it Dual Imagery.

Each of us experiences inner conflict many times a day. Often we battle the desire of the moment because of guilt, or fear, or our sense of responsibility. This can be seen in different people's behavior when they must choose between going to a motion picture which they very much want to see and completing some urgent work. One person will go to the movie and feel guilty about neglecting his job. Another will go and blame his superior for assigning too much work. A third will remain in his office and feel inadequate because he has not kept up his assignment. A fourth will give up the movie, do his work, feel proud of his superior dedication to the activities of the organization, and then go home and become irrationally angry at his wife. Of course, there are many other possible responses.

Let's do a Dual Image:

(Remember, closing your eyes and relaxing will definitely aid the flow of your imagery. Trust yourself and just let it happen.)

I'd like you to imagine two different animals.

When you have visualized these two animals, take a fresh sheet of paper and write the name of one on the upper left side and the other on the upper right side.

Write down the best word you can think of to describe each.

Now imagine these two animals walking down a road together.

Let yourself go and allow the movie to unfold before you, then write down what you imagined. Remember, your imagery must precede your writing.

Next, imagine a statement from one animal to the other and the other's answer.

Write down the two statements.

Now reverse the procedure so the animal that answered speaks first this time, and then have the other reply.

Does your imagery begin to have meaning?

What kinds of feelings are connected to each animal? What kinds of emotions do you experience while watching their interaction? How do you feel about the dialogue?

The intensity of feeling associated with the images may indicate how strong the conflict is, or make you more aware of the conflict and how important it is in your life. If the opposition is extreme between *any two* images, you may feel guilt and anxiety.

I find that the two animals express one of the different ways that conflict is experienced. They often represent two parts of ourselves in conflict. Sometimes they reveal a conflict between ourselves and some other person. At other times the conflict is between an old part of ourselves, or way of behaving, and a new part of ourselves and a new way of behaving.

An example of a conflict between two parts of yourself is what you feel when you are on a diet and you are tempted to eat that piece of chocolate cake. You are caught between wanting to do the "right" thing–stick to your diet–and doing something that you would enjoy but which would make you feel guilty.

The two animals may indicate a conflict between you and someone else. It may involve disobeying an order. You felt this kind of conflict as a child when your mother told you not to stop at the hamburger joint on your way home from school, but you went anyway. As an adult you are often in conflict with others to various degrees: when you want to go to the beach for a holiday and your spouse wants to go to the mountains; when you want to drive eighty miles an hour on the freeway and the law says the limit is fifty-five; when you set a midnight curfew for your children and they stay out until 1:00 A.M.; when you would like to murder someone and the Ten Commandments say no.

The two animals can also be old and new parts of yourself. Perhaps most of your life you have responded to the demands of others by being compliant. As you matured you learned to be more assertive in certain situations. When you revert to your old pattern of behaving in a compliant manner, though you know you would feel better asserting yourself, you are wrestling with the old and the new strategies.

Dual Imagery makes you aware of conflict and its degree, and it helps you to recognize the nature of your conflict. In Chapter VII, I will show you how to use this awareness of your conflicts to resolve them. As you can see, most conflicts are the result of differences between self-definition and how we are defined by others.

As children we are told by the significant people in our lives how to act, what to do, what to say, even what to feel. We are so small and helpless, so ignorant and innocent, we can only trust those important others to know more than we do. If they say we are good and we feel bad, we try to make ourselves over to be the kind of person those others see us to be. We develop all manner of strategies to define ourselves as they define us.

All through our lives we search for our real identity. We are constantly redefining our self-image. But we never get a chance to develop our true self completely because we are constantly being defined by others; we are given an "alien" identity which we feel we must maintain. The divergence between how we feel we *should* be and how we really *want* to be can easily produce the gnawing conflict of a personality divided against itself. Our image of ourselves is always contaminated by what others see in us and ascribe to us.

Those others have enormous power over us because we see them as necessary to fulfill two basic needs. All of us need to make a difference to someone, and all of us need confirmation of ourselves; to be acknowledged. In order to fulfill these needs we adopt strategies that will make others notice us and care about us.

An old popular song "Paper Doll" shows how a young man attempts to cope with the basic needs—to make a difference and to receive confirmation:

I'm gonna buy a paper doll that I can call my own,
A doll that other fellas cannot steal.
And then those flirty, flirty guys
With their flirty, flirty eyes
Will have to flirt with dollies that are real.
When I come home at night she will be waiting.
She'll be the truest doll in all the world.
I'd rather have a paper doll that I can call my own
Than have a fickle-minded real, live girl.

These two basic needs lead to a myriad of strategies. A few years ago a London tabloid, *News of the World*, carried a story about a young man who went to neurotic extremes to satisfy his need to be important to anybody.

> I found the hoaxer, 22-year-old Douglas Sugden, at his home in Swinnow-Terrace, Stanningley, near Leeds.
>
> Lounging in an arm chair, he said, "It all seems a bit unreal now. But looking back, I realized I was trying to draw attention to myself. I know now it was a stupid, wicked thing to do. But at the time I didn't care.
>
> "I felt as if my whole life had been dominated by other people: parents, teachers, bosses, the whole system.
>
> "I wanted people to respect me. I wanted to be talked about. I was sick of being nothing but a tiny cog in a giant machine.
>
> "The double shooting came along and I was talked about all right. But not the way I wanted. I'd worked at the factory where it happened and knew the dead watchmen.
>
> "Something clicked in my mind. I got up at 1:00 A.M. the day after the murders, went down-

stairs, hit myself over the head with a milk bottle and raised the alarm.

"All hell broke loose. Police, reporters, and TV men began swarming all over the place.

". . . But I understand what goes on in the minds of people who carry out hoaxes. They are crying out for help. They want to feel important even if it's only for a moment."

The strategies we use with others serve as the source of many of our conflicts. As long as these conflicts remain unresolved, they will recur in other aspects of our lives and will continue to be a source of anxiety, fear, panic, or guilt.

Take a little time now to re-examine your two-animal image, the interaction and the dialogue, to see if they reveal any of the opposites that occur in most of our lives. Look for a conflict between dominant or passive behavior, between security situations and risk-taking, between resistance actions and growth actions. Is there a conflict between your real self and your alien self? Between "good you" and "bad you"? Between the new self and the old self?

Your conflict may be seen as the self *versus* the self, yet invariably the self that represents a neurotic side is also representative of how you have been falsely defined by others. The unhealthy side is really the opinion of a significant other which you have accepted and internalized as "bad me."

We all have some form of conflict in our lives. A person totally free of any conflict would be in suspended animation. Many times a day we choose between two courses of action. However, as Karen Horney wrote in *Our Inner Conflicts*, "The neurotic person is not free to choose. He is driven by equally compelling forces in opposite directions neither of which he wants to follow."

Dual Imagery can tell us a great deal about whether the conflict is equally strong on both sides or if, perhaps, the healthier side can win. Always look for the outstanding difference between the two images. Even if the images seem to be virtually the same, I strongly suggest you search for some difference. Conflicts are often subtle and not immediately discernible.

Also check to determine the extent of the conflict. In asking you to visualize two different animals, I am suggesting one of the simplest Dual Imagery sequences. Such a sequence does not absolutely guarantee opposites, but most times two opposing forces within the imager's framework of experience will emerge.

If the images seem 180 degrees apart, they are as opposite as they can get. That means strong conflict—two forces in opposition, neither of which wants to give. For example, visualizing a deer and a cow suggest far less conflict than if the images are a tiger and a mouse. By nature the deer and the cow are not so different, but there is a vast difference between a mouse and a tiger.

When you examine your images for degree of conflict, you are looking at opposing elements within yourself. The classic example of conflict between opposite elements is the schism between good and evil in the protagonist of Robert Louis Stevenson's novel, *Dr. Jekyll and Mr. Hyde.* The book's theme is the idea of separating the conflicting elements in man. "From an early date," says Dr. Jekyll, ". . . I had learned to dwell with pleasure, as a beloved daydream, on the thought of separation of these elements. If each, I told myself, could but be housed in separate identities, life would be relieved of all that was unbearable." But even in a story they could not successfully be separated because they were two forces within the same person—complementary opposites.

On the other hand, separation or polarization is not possible unless conflict between two forces exists. In his novel, *The Star Rover*, Jack London has his main character attempt to play chess games with himself while imprisoned.

> By sheer visualization under my eyelids, I constructed chessboards and played both sides of long games through to checkmate. But when I had become expert at this visualized game of memory, the exercise palled on me. Exercise it was, for there could be no real contest when the same player played both sides. I tried and tried vainly, to split my personality into two personalities and to pit one against the other. But ever I remained the one player, with no planned ruse or strategy on one side that the other side did not simultaneously apprehend.

Since the chess player could not separate himself into two opposing people, his exercises lacked the element vital to games—conflict.

When you imagine the two animals walking down the road together, the intensity and quality of their interactions give further clues to the nature and the degree of the conflicts involved.

Karen Horney said the greatest part of anxiety is the result of being helplessly caught in a dilemma, both sides of which are imperative. Dual Imagery reveals these anxiety-producing dilemmas and eventually can point a way to resolution.

Here is a Dual Image that will express the degree of bipolarization you are feeling:

Imagine *any* image that comes to you. Let it develop in your mind's eye and then say out loud what the image is.

Speaking serves to establish it clearly as a separate image.

When you have done that, imagine the *most opposite* image to that first spoken image.

Again describe the image out loud, establishing its separateness.

Now compare the two for the outstanding difference between them.

The dissimilarity between the two images reveals some aspect of internal conflict and indicates just how torn you are by that conflict.

Often the polarization is clearly between the self and another. The image produced may be a sheep and a lion, with the lion representing a boss to whom the individual reacts passively. Thus the lion defines the sheep. By accepting the lion's definition, the sheep finds himself in conflict—suppressing the real self and reacting as a sheep because the lion decrees it.

You can also compare two *different* images of the same species: two different ants or two different butterflies.

If there seem to be but small differences at first, look again. Upon careful examination they may indicate profound differences.

Make a statement to each insect and have each make a statement back to you.

Have them speak to each other.

Select an adjective for each.

It should be clear to you by now that when you are asked to imagine two different animals, trees, people, chairs, faces, or what-have-you, you are likely to present two different parts of yourself at war within you or a conflict between yourself and some other person in your life.

Here is an example of one man's imagery when he was asked to imagine two different animals in human situations:

> The poodle is of the large variety. His demeanor or swishiness on his job of interior decorating is deliberate. He figures that it's the way to sell his services to his rich clients. He is not a groomed poodle but has his natural coat. He is verbal, sensitive, fast thinking and spontaneous. When not at work he's straight. I can see him making out with female poodles or being married. If married, he'd feel upset about making out with females other than his wife but nonetheless would want to. I visualize him living in a very rich style. I feel his job behavior is an artifice to reassure the husbands of his clients since he is with their wives for many hours a day alone.
>
> I see him making out with single female clients.
>
> The tiger has no particular job, and, in fact, does not care about work at all. I see him cruising around in a convertible looking for girls. He is highly mobile. He lives in a motor home and

spends very little time in any particular place. He is highly educated but uncommunicative. He hardly talks at all but does get his point across. I see him making out with any woman he chooses, too.

The tiger is very strong but, like a tiger, walks very quietly. He appears almost comically gentle and cute. However, when out in the woods just being a tiger, I can see him running down a deer with powerful tigerlike speed. After taking the deer he looks quite fierce.

I feel the tiger verbalizes very little, being preoccupied with direct existence. If he's reading a book, he looks fierce. I see him looking cute only when he's looking for some pussy.

I can contrast the two:

Poodle	*Tiger*
Verbal	Quiet
Spontaneous	Deliberate
Work-oriented	Being
Self-critical	Confident
Protective of others	Himself first
Self-effacing	Directly strong
Concerned with others' image of him	Uses images to gain what he wants
Unable to insist on defining himself	Cannot be defined by others
Conscience-stricken	Amoral
Defiant	Accepting
Competitive	Gets what he wants independently
Non-deserving	Cares about himself
In pain	At ease
Timid	Courageous
Little	Big
Choked up	Flowing
	Gambles

As to how the above relates to me, I can see myself as more of a poodle than a tiger. I see the poodle's behavior as being a way of not competing while at the same time wanting to compete. Most of his mind's time is concerned with what others see him as being. Basically the poodle is scared. Self-acknowledgment is impossible for him. This explains his swishiness on the job since he can say to himself, "I'm not a good decorator; people hire me to get their kicks laughing at me." Here swishiness equals self-effacement.

I can see poodle behavior in me all the time.

As for how the tiger relates to me? In my job I'm a tiger at times. I would feel better about myself being a tiger. The poodle in me sees the tiger as being selfish and unconcerned about others. The tiger denies himself nothing that he wants. He lives continually in the "ground of being." This gives him his appeal and strength. Like other cats he always falls on his feet in any situation.

Even though I hope I'm a tiger, I'm still poodle enough to feel panicky about seeing my tiger side and even more afraid to be the tiger. The bullshit is that I always see a division between being what I want to be and doing what I *should do* [Horney's tyranny of the "should"]. This last line is pure poodle. The tiger would never consider any action in which being and doing were conflicted and if someone or thing got in his way, he'd use a swipe of his paw to knock it out of his way.

If personalities had size, the poodle would be two feet high where the tiger would be as big as a mountain.

Dual Imagery with a person who has resolved his internal conflicts will not appear as polarized. The essential difference between the two images may be minimal. For example, a fifty-year-old man who had resolved a host of problems and seemed very much at ease was asked to imagine that he held something different in each hand. His right hand held a rose and his left hand, Indian beads. I asked him to have each of the images say something to him. The remarks were gentle and warm from both the rose and the beads. His answers to each were similar. I then asked him to bring them together. He did, and placing them over his heart, he seemed to flow with the peaceful imagery in a relaxed manner.

Now try another exercise.

Take two sheets of paper and draw a different tree on each sheet.

Write an adjective for each, and write what each tree would say to the other.

Write what each tree would say to you.

How do you feel about the trees?

Draw the trees from your imagery. The artistic quality is not essential—all that matters is that you feel free enough to draw. I ask you to draw this time so that you can have a permanent picture of your images which will be clearer than those that are verbalized or written.

Look at the papers in front of you to help you gain some idea of what your images, drawing, and statements mean.

How do these drawings of your images relate to your life?

What are they telling you about where you are right now?

What are they telling you about the future?

At some later time you may want to look at the pictures again, and perhaps you will note other aspects not seen at this time. You can also redo the drawing of the same images a few months later. At that time you can compare differences or similarities. When you redo the exercise, it is best not to look at the original drawing until the second set is completed.

Drawing or painting images is a fertile avenue of self-exploration when you follow the guiding principles of Dual Imagery.

I have suggested two trees because artistic ability is minimally required and is less apt to intimidate people who feel inhibited about drawing. I urge everyone to try the two trees even if you feel initial resistance. Bear in mind that you are doing this for yourself. You are not going to enter the pictures in an art show, nor do you need to show them to anyone else. And who knows, you may discover hidden talent!

Those who can free themselves from restraint can go on to draw the two different animals visualized earlier. After you have done the adjective for each and the statements back and forth, you can then make a single drawing of the two animals walking down a road together.

Remember, the above exercise involving the two animals is for those who are *not* inhibited by drawing. If drawing inhibits the free flow of imagery, if you freeze at the sight of a blank sheet of paper, I suggest you stick to verbalizing and writing down your imagery.

If, however, you are adventurous, the attempt to draw may be helpful. When nonverbal people have difficulty expressing the meaning imagery has for them, they often find that drawing the images frees them a little and can provide a therapeutic experience.

Drawing also "nails down" the image, reducing the chance of having the whole experience denied. It is there, concrete, for you to peruse. You can absorb the value of the images without being influenced by the judgments of others.

For a change of pace, let's play a little game called "Ping and Pong." Don't look for rhyme or reason. Just look around you and call whatever you see either "ping" or "pong." This is strictly subjective and intuitive. There are no rights or wrongs.

Suppose you see hot soup and ice cream. Which would be ping and which would be pong? To me, at least, ice cream is ping and hot soup is pong. If ping and pong were all we had to name an elephant and a cat, which would you call which? I think the answer is clear. Or is it?

This concept seems the simplest medium in which relationships between two things can be expressed. It doesn't always work—two words are insufficient to categorize all relationships, yet ping and pong somehow seem to lend themselves to an infinity of dichotomies. We may not always agree, but almost any two things can be expressed by these categories and they suggest something about the way each of us sees the world. There is an internal consistency in each person's replies, so there will probably also be a consistency in our disagreements.

Such classifications make an amusing party game, but there are far deeper implications for the fascinating world of imagery. E. H. Gombrich, the English art critic, says in *Art and Illusion* that we may be talking playful nonsense or serious nonsense. So while it may be merely playful to say that Rembrandt is pong and Watteau is ping, or that pretty women are ping and matrons are pong, there is a serious aspect in the high percentage of agreement on these classifications. They are but another way of expressing a constantly recurring principle of organization within us all—duality or opposition.

Furthermore, when comparing any two objects, persons, or creatures, one is seen as brighter, or higher, or lighter. Gombrich tells us how Professor Roman Jacobson, a linguist, found a high level of agreement to the statement that *i* is brighter than *u*. While there are actually solid linguistic facts to verify this impression, the important point is that we do not need any profound knowledge of linguistics to respond. So if we say the step from *u* to *i* is more like an upward step than a downward step, there would be a consensus regardless of what explanations are offered.

Quite independently, and before I had heard of Gombrich's and Jacobson's ping and pong, I had developed my concept of Dual Imagery. My major interest was psychotherapy and not art, yet I was aware of the same type of relationships. The binary principle seems to be deeply rooted in the human psyche. Philosophers, from the ancient Greek, Heraclitus, to Hegel in the nineteenth century, have conceded that words and concepts derive their meaning in relation to their opposites. "X" means something relative to "non X." Thus it is not surprising that in all languages we can study words which can be set forth in pairs of complementary opposites, e.g. dark and light; hot and cold; good and bad—the number is limitless. The central theme is that of polarity or opposition. Even digital computers use binary opposition—they function in either the "on" or the "off" position and everything can be expressed with two digits: "1" and "0."

To continue our discussion of Dual Imagery:

Imagine the image inside of you and then the image outside of you.

Now have the image on the inside say something to the image on the outside.

Then have the outside image say something to the image on the inside.

Is there some sort of struggle between them? Are these two parts of you at war?

Are you getting meaning from these images? How much emotion are you feeling about each image?

Still another way of seeing the inside and outside of you is to imagine the spit in your mouth. I suspect you would say, "Okay, it's in my mouth. So what?"

So—imagine spitting your saliva into a glass of water. The spit from inside of you is now outside of you and in a glass of water. Can you imagine drinking the contents of the glass? My guess is that you would have as much difficulty imagining drinking the water containing spit as you would have in actually doing it. Some of you may feel and show disgust at such a prospect. Yet only a short moment before you were not disgusted with the spit inside your mouth.

A similar transformation of feelings toward other inner images or substances may occur if they are seen outside the body. This applies as well to feces or undigested food. Try to discover why the images are transformed when they are removed from your body and exposed to observation.

Here is another observational experiment which may seem at first like a simple parlor game but which can supply further information about you. Would you believe that your eye movements while you are actively engaged in doing imagery or any concentrated task may indicate something about you?

You will need a partner for the following exercise. Using your partner's nose as the center, concentrate on the right eye. When the partner is asked to divide 4,675 by 27 without paper or pencil you will notice that the eye will move laterally. It may move toward the nose (left) or toward the temple (right). If the first attempt doesn't work, try asking your partner how many letters there are in the word "anthropology" and check for right or left movement of the right eye. Be sure you do *not* tell your partner that you are observing eye movements.

Any complex question that requires a person to pause and reflect will do. Long mathematical problems to be done in the head or questions about how many letters in words like "hippopotamus" are appropriate. You will not get the results you seek if you ask the other person to spell "but" or to add two plus two.

Those persons who move their right eye to the left more than seven out of ten times are considered "left-movers"; if the eye moves right, they are "right-movers." David Bakan reported in an article in *Perceptual and Motor Skills* that 70 per cent of the time he could classify subjects as either left- or right-movers.

Several investigators have determined that right- and left-movers have distinct personality characteristics. The left-mover is controlled by the right hemisphere of the brain which is largely responsible for creativity, imagination, and artistic and musical ability. The right-mover is predominantly involved with analytic, logical thinking, particularly in mathematical and verbal functions.

Among the characteristics ascribed to each are:

Left-mover	*Right-mover*
nonverbal	verbal
emotional	rational
upper visceral activity	lower visceral activity
more vivid imagery	digital, numerical
subjective	objective
prone to asthma	prone to migraine
passive	active
high hypnotic susceptibility	low hypnotic susceptibility
on SAT, higher score on verbal skills	on SAT, higher score mathematical skills
music, religion	

Left-movers tend toward "soft" majors in college—humanities, psychology, political science, English, history, international relations, nursing, and communications. Right-movers seem to gravitate to mathematics, biology, engineering, economics, and physics.

There is no relationship between left and right movement and left- or right-handedness. Nor is there a relationship between eye movement and gender. For some reason, a high percentage of married couples show opposite eye movement directions.

It may be interesting to check out eye movements among your friends to see if the artists, musicians, and ministers are left-movers and the accountants and engineers are right-movers. If you are a job analyst or a personnel manager, you may even entertain the idea of using eye movement to determine where an applicant would be most effectively placed. Perhaps that sounds a bit far-fetched, yet when we consider some of the associations attached to the concepts of right and left, you may be more receptive to the suggestion.

The opposition of right and left is one of the primary examples of duality. The left and right sides of ourselves seem to have different meanings for us. The consensus, historically and in almost all cultures, characterizes the left as weak, feminine, unclean; and the right as strong, masculine, and clean. Many psychoanalysts consider the left to be associated with the female principle and with the emotions. In most religions, in mysticism, and in magic, the left is the side of evil. The invoked devil is always shown in medieval paintings leaving the magic circle with the left hand outstretched. The left hand is considered unlucky.

The opposition of left and right is also expressed in language. "Sinister" means left in Latin. The Anglo-Saxon "lyft" means weak or worthless. In Italian "mancino" (left-handed) means treacherous and dishonest. There are numerous other examples.

Many Eastern people consider the left hand to be unclean—to be used only to wipe excretion and for making love, i.e. caressing.

Right-handedness is predominant in all aggressive and/or predatory species. Chimps and gorillas are ambidextrous and are essentially fruit and nut eaters, while rats and lobsters are right dominant and aggressive.

For whatever it means, women button their coats to the left and men button theirs to the right.

Theodore Blau, in a paper given at an American Psychological Association meeting, concluded that left-handed children are more imaginative than right-handed children, although only about 5 per cent of all children are left-handed. I can't state categorically that left-handed people are the most creative, but there seems to be some indication that they have an edge on right-handers. The ancient cave drawings are believed to have been done by left-handed people. Furthermore, such famous persons as Leonardo Da Vinci, Michelangelo, Goethe, Nietzsche, and Beethoven were all left-handed.

Take a moment to image something in your left hand and something in your right hand.

Can you categorize them according to the principles we have been discussing?

You may be puzzled to find that they do not seem to conform to the pattern. It varies.

I cannot tell you whether the associations with the left and the right are biologically or culturally induced. I suspect that there is a large element of both involved, and there is also a correlation with the known hemispheric functions of the brain, in the same way that eye movements have such a correlation. It is also a fact that the human body is asymmetrical. The right lung, for instance, has three ventricles, and the left lung has only two. The same asymmetry is found in other organs. Therefore, the center of gravity is slightly to the right of center.

In addition to the polarization between left and right, we metaphorically extend the principles of duality to other dimensions. "Back," "front," "up," and "down" have symbolic meanings. Height and up are generally associated with heaven, angels, achievement; low and down suggest bad, evil, hell. The route to the unconscious is backward and downward.

Let's look at the symbolism of "front" and "back." Close your eyes and take your time.

Imagine an image in front of you and then imagine an image behind you.

Now imagine *you are each image* in turn. *As the image*, finish the following sentences:

I feel______________________________.
I secretly__________________________.
I need______________________________.
I will______________________________.

What do the image in front and the image behind mean to you?

Experience indicates that the image in front refers most often to things of the future or what is ahead literally. And so, conversely, the image behind in most instances refers to the past or literally what is behind us. Do you see meaning in the opposition of these forces?

A patient when asked to imagine looking through a telescope often sees the future or how it might be. When asked to imagine looking into the same telescope which is turned 180 degrees around from its original position, the image viewed is of the past or that which is behind.

In psychotherapy, at times it is possible to determine the optimism or pessimism of the patient by what is imaged ahead or in front. And often that which is imaged behind is negative and can be heavily laden with conflict or even violence.

The poet, Robert Frost, has been described as unsure of himself and chronically suspicious of his surroundings. A backward glance, an anxious look over the shoulder, was habitual as he constantly assessed his situation. Do you do the same thing?

Imagine you are walking down a road and somebody taps you on the shoulder from behind.

How do you feel?

Say something to that person.

What does the person say to you?

Look for some meaning in the interactions. This imaginary situation oftentimes relates to strong forces outside ourselves. It can also be a clue to inner conflicts.

In myths it is the devil who dogs our footsteps on the lonely path and for whom one may not look back. Lot's wife became a pillar of salt when she looked back. Orpheus lost the reclaimed Eurydice to the underworld for a second time and forever when he looked back to see if she was following him. Jesus said, "Get thee behind me, Satan," i.e. back to your proper place.

Here is one of the most complex imaginary situations I use. Spend as much time as you like on this image, and note in detail what is on the right, on the left, and in front and in back of you. Do not expect to understand all the ramifications of this image at once. You may want to go back to it many times until you have elicited all of the complexities involved:

You are in the center of four walls. Each wall is ten feet by ten feet. You are to imagine something on each wall.

The "Four Walls," as an imaginary situation, can be more enlightening for specific individuals than any other I have been able to observe. Let's see what it can do for you.

I originally contended that this image could reveal the "being in the world" of an individual. Indeed, for some persons this is an adequate explanation and does quite verifiably represent the person's "world view." However, the usual symbolic predictability of the front view as the future and the back view as the past does not always apply to this image. No specific pattern of predictability seems to occur in contrasting right and left sides. Yet despite the lack of predictability, the material elicited can be of the most unique and meaningful, and sometimes the most powerful, of any imaginary situation offered.

This image often leads to past memory images. Imagery that reveals previously undetected conflict may be seen on some of the walls. To develop this kind of imagery, ask yourself at which wall you would care to spend the most time and at which wall you would care to spend the least time.

One wall may be more emotionally charged for you than the others. You may want to imagine entering the wall, and continue the imagery. This may help you clarify conflicts, recognize significant areas of defensiveness, and become aware of characteristic styles of behavior. The variations are enormous. Be prepared to use your creativity as your image reveals heretofore undetected conflicts and feelings. Don't be afraid to go where your images take you.

Here is how a twenty-four-year-old woman responded to the Four Walls imagery:

At the left: A forest with lots of tall trees and greenery.
Statement from image: "Come inside and find me."
In front: Big canvas painting with some splattering on it.
Statement from image: "You are always waving back and forth."
On the right: Something splattered against the wall —almost black.
Statement from image: "You're dead."
Behind: A little box like a peephole.
Statement from image: "I'm going to frustrate you."

She then said, "I keep looking forward to that canvas—the one with the splattering on it."

When I asked her at which wall she would like

to spend the most time, it was at the left with the forest and trees. She said she would spend the least time in the one behind her where there was a little box with the peephole.

I then asked her to enter the right wall. She responded, "I see a long box like a coffin with pastel satin inside (she laughs strongly) and a light shining over it. I'm always a martyr. My mother called me a martyr and said I was too dramatic. Mother could have died in one of her epileptic convulsions; I always was afraid of what we children would do if she did, and what my responsibility would be. Also I get a view of my grandfather's funeral."

Following this, she entered the forested left wall and said, "It's cool and refreshing. It's full of potential. I'm going to find new things. I'll find a cabin. It gives me feelings of growth and growing."

When I asked her to enter the front wall she imagined, "My life the way it's been. To draw circles extending out. When I used crayons, as a kid, I would draw wavy lines over the page. It's like my life crossing lines–wavy–going from the Chicano life into other ways of life."

The strongest imagery occurred when I asked her to enter the rear wall. At first she couldn't and said all she could do was look through the peephole. A few moments later she said, "I can do it now," and she imagined entering the real wall. "I see a kitchen table that's bright, but it's dark all around it. It reminds me of the table we had in our kitchen. Sometimes it looks big. It's the old-fashioned chrome kind with dishes on it. Silverware and food in bowls. Now it changes to one place setting. I walk up to it and sit down and look to the left to a door. It's dark behind the door, and it leads to my old bedroom. My door never opened all the way, so you could see and hear things secretly. We could never say what we really thought. It was the house my mother and father got divorced in. I remember now, suddenly, my high school days. They were dreadfully unhappy. Mother was sick there. She had epilepsy. When she had seizures, I was blamed. I remember painting the four rooms to cover up the misery. It's a house I cried in a lot and got slapped around in. I was told how I must behave. My father lectured me about becoming a lesbian because my aunt was, and I liked her. I never knew what a lesbian was. My aunt, who was one, moved to San Francisco, and when I threatened to leave, they thought I would join her. I'm not a lesbian, but they kept thinking I was going to be one because I liked my aunt's freedom."

You can see what powerful feelings and associations can come to light with this imagery. I find that usually one wall will be most emotionally charged and will lead to powerful uncovering of reminiscent imagery comingled with present-day experiences. It can lead to an awareness of historical self-images—how a person saw himself at some time in the past. Often significant people in the imager's life are revealed more easily than they would be under direct questioning.

The Four Walls is nearly always a rich source of meaningful material.

Sometimes it is easier to see needs we cannot accept in ourselves expressed by other people. This may account for the universal interest in classic dramas in which men are divided against themselves. Some of the popularity of *Oedipus Rex* or *King Lear* or *Hamlet* must reflect the fact that the primary characters are struggling with conflicts which have plagued all people through time.

Often the theme of conflict has earned for the artist or philosopher a popular appeal that he might not have had otherwise. Because of St. Augustine's struggles with "lust of the flesh, lust of the eyes, and pride," he is far better known to the layman than is Aquinas, who was his superior as a formal philosopher. Similarly, Hogarth and Dostoevsky provide unique interest with their portrayals of self-torment and depravity.

The vicarious experiencing of conflicting needs is as frequently a goal in the applied arts as it is in the fine arts. A semiclothed model in a seductive pose suggests that the use of Brand-X soap or Brand-Y toothpaste will resolve the conflicts arising from unfulfilled needs. Some of the most popular detective stories seem to sell because of their bone-crushing, face-smashing sadism. Soap operas help many housewives escape from their drab existence by letting them live vicariously the exciting lives of the heroines. There is little doubt that the commercial potency of such appeals derives from the imaginary fulfillment of needs that have few other real expressions.

Conflict is required for tragedy, and tragedy is the tool of the writer who wishes to portray the character of a man. Lancelot is caught between his love for Guinevere and his devotion to King Arthur; Lady Macbeth is torn between ambition and guilt. Don Jose can have Carmen only if he betrays his country; and Faust must choose between his thirst for knowledge and eternal damnation. Popular stereotypes of famous heroes focus on their characteristic reactions to conflict: Hamlet's introspection, Peer Gynt's escape from problems through wanderlust, and the young George Washington by his honesty.

Psychologists have noted that there are close connections between a person's characteristic methods of resolving conflict and other areas of his behavior. A man who keeps his emotions in order as a means of controlling his aggression is also likely to be concerned with having his desk in order, keeping appointments at the exact time, and maintaining a detailed budget. Or, if he is inclined to attribute to others the anger that he cannot tolerate in himself, his suspiciousness may lead him to be unduly secretive about his personal affairs, very sensitive to the motives of others, and preoccupied with methods of avoiding trouble. He is not usually an enthusiastic or outgoing person.

There are hundreds of clinical cases which illustrate the connections between reactions to conflict and such varied forms of behavior as the jokes a person tells, his dreams and fantasies, the patterns of his doodles, his vocational interests, his styles of physical expression, or his reactions to the threat of failure. In view of the connection among these types of behavior, Wilhelm Reich long ago suggested that techniques for resolving conflicts form the nucleus of a "character structure."

Dual Imagery, as I have presented it, can help you to reveal conflict areas in your life. It can suggest your characteristic patterns of resolving or avoiding conflict; can suggest which conflicts are easily resolved and which are deeply rooted and may require further help; can show the value of conflict in your life; and can help you clarify and deal with your private world view and your interrelationships within that world.

CHAPTER IV

Looking at Yourself Looking at Yourself

How we think of ourselves—as competent or incompetent, attractive or repulsive, honest or dishonest—has a tremendous effect on our behavior in different situations.

All of us have a theory of ourselves, about what kind of person we are. This theory is called the self-image or self-concept. We can observe ourselves more clearly and understand our self-concept more fully through the medium of imagery—the Self-Image experience.

Let's start with such an imagery:

Imagine that there are *two* of you and that one of you is sitting on your lap.

How does it feel?

What was difficult or easy about this image?

Your feeling reaction to this imagery in self-observation probably revealed an attitude you have about yourself.

Do you like yourself?

Despise yourself?

Like one part of you but not another part?

Would you like to make some changes?

Or are you satisfied with who and what you are?

To get further into Self-Imagery, try this exercise:

Imagine that there are two of you and imagine hugging yourself.

Do you feel warm and loving?

Is it difficult to imagine hugging yourself?

Take your time and let the imagery develop with all the attendant feelings and actions. It may be profitable to record your feelings and reactions to these imageries.

Were you surprised by your feelings about yourself?

Were there important differences between sitting on your lap and hugging yourself?

In doing these two imageries did you become aware of things in yourself you did not suspect? Both of these exercises may enhance your understanding of yourself, your feelings of warmth and intimacy with yourself, and may reveal some of your defenses.

When you have finished exploring these two imageries, try the following exercise:

Imagine there are two of you, and imagine holding your own face in your hands.

What feelings are you having?

Is there a difference between feeling and being felt?

Did you hold your face tenderly and look deeply into your eyes?

How did you like the feel of your hands on your face?

Perhaps you were unable to do this imagery. Sometimes this image may lead to feelings of shame and guilt, to old binds, or to the recollection of traumatic incidents in your past. Did this particular image add further dimensions to what you felt and learned when you sat on your lap and when you hugged yourself?

Certain key times in the course of your life may be connected with a specific self-concept. Then later, when changes have taken place in your life, your self-concept will change to a new self-definition. In order for you to know yourself, you need a clear conception of how you have defined yourself in the past and how you are now defining yourself. Sometimes self-definition may be hazy and elusive, but when you imagine hugging yourself, sitting on your own lap, or holding your own face in your hands, you may have clarity thrust upon you.

Whether or not you realize it, you possess a series of principles for organizing the way you see yourself, the world around you, and how you fit into it. Your self-definition is central to most of your activities. Sometimes there is a transition between old self-definitions and new, emerging self-definitions. Awareness of the contrast between these two can serve as a guide and can help make change possible.

Let us consider an example. A young man's self-definition in his last year of high school was one of shyness, self-doubt, and shaky masculinity. By the time he had finished his university training, he had worked out a great many of his problems, and his self-definition changed to one of confidence and strong masculinity. Old self-concepts had given way to new self-concepts.

On the other hand, when solid and positive self-concepts change to negative ones, behavior is guided by embarrassment, shame, and guilt. At these times anxiety or panic may be felt. Often traumatic incidents may trigger these feelings.

Alberto Moravia in *A Ghost at Noon* describes his change of self-image:

> I was so troubled, at that period, that even the image I had hitherto made of myself in my own mind had changed. Up till then I had looked upon myself as an intellectual, a man of culture, a writer for the theater—the "art" theater, I mean—for which I had always had a great passion and to which I felt I was drawn by a natural vocation. This *moral* image, as I may call it, also had an influence on the *physical* image: I saw myself as a young man whose thinness, short sight, nervousness, pallor, and carelessness in dress all bore witness, in anticipation, to the literary glory for which I was destined. But at that time, under the

> pressure of my cruel anxieties, this very promising and flattering picture had given place to an entirely different one, that of a poor devil who had been caught in a shabby, pathetic trap, who had not been able to resist his love for his wife and had overreached himself and would be forced to struggle, for goodness knows how much longer, in the mortifying toils of poverty.

William C. Lewis in his book, *Why People Change*, gives a clear example of how waking imagery revealed changes in self-concept for a man in psychotherapy:

> A professor reacted with feelings of reflection and disconfirmation to an administrative change in his responsibilities in a fashion he recognized as completely inappropriate. He felt sudden and profound depression for no reason, in his own opinion. He experienced many somatic symptoms including continual retching and pain in the upper abdomen and lower chest. His wife's reaction in early co-therapy hours seemed callous—she chided him for his overreaction and shamed him. When he was urged to "make a waking dream" about the pain—to go where his fantasies took him—he thought of a huge bird ripping at his entrails, of his terror and wish to escape from this crushing, devouring assault by a quick suicidal death, and then switched suddenly to another subject. He began to talk of his feelings when he was placed in a foundling home for a time when eighteen months old, following the death of his father. As he continued to talk, an abrupt change occurred in his nonverbal communication. He had come into therapy appearing to be like the proverbial cigar-store Indian, carved out of

> wood. Before his depression he had usually presented a casual but jaunty Mississippi River gambler "front." Now, as his fantasy took him back to times charged for him with terror and reactive fury, he began to weep. His therapists felt him hover and waver between abreaction and defensive denial. He first wept, then pulled himself together, speaking of present real problems, then wept again more profusely, then minimized, and so on. One could infer that his wife's coolness stemmed in part from his covert instructions over the years to her to help him reinforce his defensive avoidance of feelings he had had to surmount when very young. In the therapy hour during her husband's account of his fantasy a perceptive softening and warming in her attitude took place. The content of the fantasy itself (regarding the rapacious bird) was not examined during this hour at all. The aspects of this man's waking fantasy which brought therapeutic movement were his inner archaic anguish, his struggle to minimize it, and his wife's response. . . .

For the sake of clarity I want to explain the key concept of self-definition now. Please bear in mind at all times that how we define ourselves is never separate from how others define us. Our self-definition is inextricably tied to how we feel others perceive us. Even when we are alone, our thinking, images, and behavior always relate to other people, real and imaginary.

How many times have you caught yourself doing something because you know it will please someone you care about? How often do you do things in a certain way because that significant other has said that is how it should be done? Certainly, you have refrained from behaving in a certain way or have altered your behavior for the same reason. And just as certainly, you have become aware of what you were doing because you realized it was really not *your* way and, furthermore, the other would probably never even know you were doing it.

At those times you were in touch with your own image of yourself, with the image you felt the other had of you, and with your image of the other person. You were conscious at that moment of the tangled web of interrelationships that direct us all.

The observation of others are frequently valuable ones, as they potentially carry rich data about you and your development.

Sartre in his autobiography, *The Words*, shows this point clearly:

> My truth, my character, and my name were in the hands of adults. I had learned to see myself through their eyes....
>
> ... I was an impostor. How can one put on an act without knowing that one is acting? The clear, sunny semblances that constituted my role were exposed by a lack of being which I could neither quite understand nor cease to feel. I would turn to the grown-ups, I would ask them to guarantee my merits. In doing so, I sank deeper into the imposture. Condemned to please, I endowed myself with charms that withered on the spot. Everywhere I went, I dragged about my false good nature, my idle importance, on the alert for a new opportunity. When I thought that I had seized it, I would strike a pose only to find once again the hollowness which I was trying to get away from. My grandfather would be dozing, wrapped in his plaid blanket. Under his bushy

moustache I would see the pink nakedness of his lips. It was unbearable. Luckily his glasses would slide off. I would rush to pick them up. He would awaken, would lift me in his arms, we would play our big love scene. It was no longer what I had wanted. What had I wanted? I would forget everything. I would make my nest in the thicket of his beard. I would go into the kitchen, would declare that I wanted to dry the salad. There would be cries and giggles: "No, darling, not like that. Squeeze your little hand tighter. That's right! Marie, help him. But he's doing very well." I was a fake child, I was holding a fake salad washer. I could feel my acts changing into gestures. Play-acting robbed me of the world and of human beings. I saw only roles and props. Serving the activities of adults in a spirit of buffoonery, how could I have taken their worries seriously? I adapted myself to their intentions with a virtuous eagerness that kept me from sharing their purposes. A stranger to the needs, hopes, and pleasures of the species. I squandered myself coldly in order to charm it. It was my audience. I was separated from it by footlights that forced me into a proud exile which quickly turned to anguish.

Worst of all, I suspected the adults of faking. The words they spoke to me were candies, but they talked among themselves in quite another tone.

There is considerable evidence to support the belief that each of us has a self-system—a set of attitudes we carry about ourselves. This is entirely interpersonal in origin and is gradually developed out of the appraisals of others. Such phrases as: "Johnny is so good-looking," "Helen is quite clumsy," or "Lisa is a clever child" are the basis of this self-system. Although the self-image evolves gradually, the security operations invoked to maintain self-respect and self-esteem are present from the very beginning. Threats to the self-esteem and self-respect are experienced as anxiety. This in turn produces defensive maneuvers to relieve that anxiety and to protect the self.

The two following imaginary situations may help to uncover some of the events in your past which contributed to the development of your self-system.

Imagine you are in a classroom. What happens? Who else is there?

This image often relates to your self-image in terms of intelligence or stupidity. It may help you to discover why you think of yourself as you do and may show you some of your strengths related to intelligence.

At other times this image may uncover traumatic incidents in the past which led to the development of self-consciousness. A disapproving or rejecting teacher may have been instrumental in the development of negative aspects of your self-image. A particularly distressing event in your early school years may have been influential throughout the rest of your life.

Imagine walking into a child's playground.

This image can reveal self-concepts related to the past and to early peer relations.

What did you do on the playground?

How did you get along with the other children there?

Were you friendly or aloof?

Did they accept or reject you?

Your feelings of acceptability or unacceptability are the outgrowth of the feelings you experienced in various situations throughout your life. The two preceding imaginary situations may help you to understand why today you can walk into a roomful of strangers and feel at ease, or why you tremble at the thought of facing all those eyes.

Harry Stack Sullivan, the originator of Interpersonal Psychiatry, said all personality development can be described as the theory of the evolution of the self and its security operations. The self-image is never static and is subject to constant change.

In effect, Harry Stack Sullivan tried to do for psychiatry what B. F. Skinner is trying to do for psychology—but with an opposite focus. Skinner wants psychology to emphasize the *animalness* of human beings—the fact that our behavior can be shaped and modified according to the same principles used to shape and modify the behavior of rats and pigeons. Harry Stack Sullivan wanted psychiatry to emphasize the *humanness* of us all—the fact that human feelings, thoughts, and values are uniquely human and have *no* counterpart at the animal level.

When we make an error, fail in what we undertake, or hurt someone needlessly, our tendency is to feel we are unique—that only we could have done something so sinful and evil. When we feel so sinful and evil, we can also feel unhuman. The aim of this therapy is to help the individual to the point where his sense of positive self-regard outweighs the sense of being worthless and unhuman.

I would like to clarify the connection between our self-image and the term "identity." Identity can be explained in terms of self-images and vice versa. In short, our identity is the composite of our self-images.

By identity I mean any image or set of images, conscious or unconscious, which an individual has of himself. The full set of images of self (total identity) refers to many aspects of the person: his appetites, his past experience, his moral qualities, his social status and role, his physical appearance, etc. The structure of that person emerges.

We all have a structural self-image, and no human being is indifferent to self-images.

Your name is a way of identifying you. You undoubtedly feel a certain sense of total connection to your name being called out loud in a group. You, and probably you alone, make such a connection.

Try this exercise:

Sound your own name out loud.

Do you get a certain feeling from it? How does it sound to you?

Do you like it?

Now try to get an image of your own name? What do you see?

As you can see, in many ways your name is basic to your identity. Your reactions to it can say a lot about your self-image. Does it disturb you when your name is misspelled or mispronounced? How do you feel when it is mocked?

What you feel and how you behave are determined by the concept you have of yourself and of your abilities. If you think you are Napoleon, you will act like Napoleon—at least according to your concept of Napoleon. This is what psychologists call the phenomenal self. This is what your imagery reveals.

Everyone has a basic need to preserve and enhance this self-image. Your concept of self is the most important part of you and serves as a reference point for your every behavior. Most people, for example, regard themselves as law-abiding citizens and act accordingly. If this were not so, chaos would certainly result.

This is an exceedingly complex subject, since your self-image is composed of all the meanings which you have about yourself and your relation to the world about you. But although it is complex, it is by no means disorganized. Rather, it is a highly organized function which operates in consistent and predictable fashion.

Thus, time after time in your interactions with others you are recognizable as the same person. You maintain a coherency both for others and for yourself. If for some reason you step out of character—present another image—you may startle or puzzle others and even yourself. Wherever you are, whatever you do, maintaining and enhancing this self is the prime objective of your existence. Frank Barron tells us, "In psychological sickness our image of ourselves blurs, the colors run, it is not integrated or beautiful." And so we expend much of our energy protecting our self-image.

The following imaginary situation is particularly good for elucidating your self-image. It is an exercise in self-confrontation.

Imagine walking in a lightly wooded area where you see a hotel.

Imagine walking through the lobby, up the staircase, and entering a room where you see yourself.

What do you see yourself doing?
What do you feel?
Say something to yourself.
What do you say back to you?

This sequence of self-confrontation through imagery may lead to surprises. Seeing yourself alone in a hotel room, you may experience yourself feeling shame, or isolation, or the feeling of being lost. Sometimes good feelings accompany this imagery. Secret feelings about yourself, that you would not ordinarily reveal, often emerge.

This image can give greater awareness of yourself and your attitudes about yourself. It may point toward a direction you want your life to take and even suggest actions to help you achieve what you desire.

There is a further imaginary situation that can expand self-awareness. Allow yourself time to follow it to its conclusion. Once again there are two of you in this image. Get in touch with the feelings of each you.

Imagine there are two of you. Imagine one of you is safe on top of a mountain. Below on a ledge is another you. Imagine the you at the top throwing a strong rope to the you on the ledge. What will happen?

How does each you feel about the outcome of the sequence?

There are people who will leave themselves on the lower ledge and walk away. Others will immediately pull themselves up to safety. Their attitude toward self-help becomes apparent. At times, the one on the ledge pulls the other down. Occasionally, the other you on the ledge is a rotten or evil side of yourself. In any case, an attitude toward yourself is often made poignantly clear.

Karen Horney did not ask patients to imagine themselves in situations. However, in developing her concept of the "idealized image" and the "despised image," she did much to clarify and define those forms of self-images which neurotically propel us. Her concepts are similar to R. D. Laing's explanation of an attributed identity—an alien identity in contrast to one's real identity.

Individuals who are falsely defined by others are inclined to adopt an appearance in total opposition to that false definition. They create "idealized" images, for example, the best parent in the world, the ultimate host, the most attentive lover. In one's heart of hearts, however, there may be little or no emotional conviction in that role. The vigilance against exposure or erosion of this idealized image is constant. At best it is a façade, a defense against the introjected unacceptable person within; it is an attempt to maintain one's position in the world although the position is a false one. The greater the idealized image, the more extensive are the security operations necessary to perpetuate it. But when one operates essentially from his true identity, the idealized image becomes more realistic; the disparity between the idealized image and the true self-image is lessened considerably. Then there is a reduction of anxiety.

Although Horney did not employ imagery techniques to awaken the patient's recognition of his self-concept images, she contributed brilliantly to the dynamics of self-imagery, specifically in her concept of the "search for glory" and the role of human imagination in its development. She writes in *Neuroses and Human Growth* of the subtle unconscious imaginings of the patient prone to such a search and describes how imagination may become distorted and counterproductive:

> The idealized image is not created in a single act of creation; once produced, it needs continued attention. For its actualization, the person must put in incessant labor by way of falsifying reality. He must turn his needs into virtues or into more than justified expectations. He must turn his intentions to be honest or considerate into the fact of being honest and considerate. The bright ideas he has for a paper make him a great scholar. His potentialities turn into factual achievements. Knowing the "right" moral values makes him a virtuous person—often, indeed, a kind of moral genius. And, of course, his imagination must work overtime to discard all the disturbing evidence to the contrary.

Now instead of offering an imaginary situation I am going to ask you to finish the sentence:

Never refer to me as____________________.

Take your time and finish the sentence as honestly as you can. Your "idealized" or "despised" image may emerge from your answer.

Among the infinitely varied responses to the sentence, "Never refer to me as ________," I have heard, "stupid," "weak," "frightened," "a housewife," "insignificant," "useless," "limited," "helpless," "woebegone," "a disgrace," "out-of-date," and "mechanical." These are really despised images.

One very extroverted, active lady replied, "Never refer to me as incompetent." When I asked her who was the most incompetent person she knew, she answered immediately, "Me!" This from a woman with two children who was teaching school and also training for a new career!

The make-believe play of children is an important part of the development of a self-system. Pretending is so common among children that we all readily accept it. As children develop, they practice a variety of make-believe selves and roles. Gradually they learn to differentiate themselves from the surrounding world and to see the many options within themselves, a greater range of trial selves. From adolescence on, these ultimately become the basis of the more solid and separate self.

Your self-image is the single most important concept in your consciousness. Right from the beginning it is not neutral, but evaluative. As a child you developed judgments about yourself. You believed yourself to be intelligent or stupid, pretty or ugly, loved or hated, worthy or unworthy. Most of your actions stemmed from your evaluations of yourself. You may have developed a negative self-image and accepted it so thoroughly that you ceased to strive for certain goals. On the other hand, you may have rejected a poor image of yourself and used your energy to overcome false definitions and to realize your potentialities.

Throughout our lives we require an accurate and acceptable self-image, and toward this end we are constantly exploring, redefining, and evaluating ourselves. Great novels and dramas have been written about these struggles for self-knowledge and self-acceptance. However, the problem is basic and universal in human experience, and not confined to just a heroic few.

Most of the time, as adults, we accept our identities without much question. It takes some unusual circumstance to focus attention on our self-image. For example, coming out of an anesthetic, we wonder who and where we are. Being alone in a foreign country can make us very aware of ourselves.

An anthropologist who had lived for a year in a small village in the New Guinea highlands told me how he awakened one morning not quite sure of who he was. Months of living among a small group of people, whose life style and language were totally alien to him, had disoriented him and had triggered self-doubts. He found himself staring into his mirror, feeling his face and body. He kept repeating his name in order to convince himself of his own identity.

The image of oneself in a mirror is often a serviceable way of reality testing. Some people when asked to see themselves in a mirror ask, "Is that really me?" They often become angry or annoyed with themselves because they see a reflection they do not like—they are too fat, too ugly, too awkward. Seeing the disliked reflection may create a "reality" that will lead to some action for change.

The mirror does not always tell the truth—it reflects our image as we perceive it. We glance into it to see if we are properly dressed, we check our grooming, but we do not usually really look at ourselves. An unexpected reflection in a shop window or in a mirrored wall may give us a moment's pause until we recognize that image as ourself. For a fleeting instant, we look at ourselves as a stranger and may see someone who differs from the picture in our mind.

Sigmund Freud tells a story of traveling in a railroad compartment and looking up to see what appeared to be a stranger in front of him. A moment later he realized that he was seeing his own reflection in the glass partition.

The mirror also validates us as a person:

> The crystal spies on us. If within the four walls of a bedroom a mirror stares, I'm no longer alone. There is someone there. In the dawn, reflections mutely stage a show.
>
> Jorge Luis Borges

Sometimes we do not need the mirror image. We create it internally. Freud and Rank refer to the concept of a "double." Rank saw the double as an insurance against the destruction of the ego, "an energetic denial of the power of death." Freud, too, believed the double was invented "as a preservation against extinction" or a protection against loss. He tells of a child who dealt with a brief separation from his mother by making his own image alternately appear and disappear in a mirror.

Association with others is necessary for validating and expanding the perception of the self by the self. They are our mirrors. When there are no human others to serve as mirrors, as in the case of those living in isolation, we invest our surroundings with imagined personalities: the prospector and his mule illustrate this need. By interacting with his mule as if it were human, the lonely prospector was able to experience many aspects of himself which could not be called forth in solitude. He used the animal as a mirror when he imagined the mule discussing and describing his actions at length. Prisoners in extended solitary confinement have been known to play the same game with spiders.

Children use imaginary companions to mirror themselves also. They fantasize other children, or animals, or adults. The imaginary companion becomes real for them and provides the feedback necessary for developing the self-image as well as a rehearsal for interactions with others. One child I know of was so convinced of the reality of her imaged friend that whenever she was taken to a restaurant, she ordered food for her imaginary companion.

Mirrors are effective in imagery also. For example:

Imagine looking at yourself in a mirror and ask yourself, "What is the most difficult thing I can say to myself?"

Take your time and concentrate on your reply. Very often your answer involves something you think you should do. Undoubtedly it is private.

Perhaps it refers to something about yourself you have wanted to change for years. It may concern a wish for the future that seems remote or impossible at this time.

The images and fantasies we have within us can motivate us into certain roles. One man who is now actively being rehabilitated at Tuum Est (a center for former drug addicts) came to the Institute for Psycho-Imagination Therapy to discuss his life as an addict. He knew he had to get forty or fifty dollars each day to support his habit, so he would start each day as if he were Humphrey Bogart or a secret agent. He would stand on the street corner with hundreds of people around him, and think how he alone knew of his mission to get money. Each policeman was someone to be avoided. Each food market was potentially a place to steal steaks to be sold "out there," or cartons of cigarettes—they sold well. Every piece of furniture in his friends' homes was a potential object to be stolen. Remarkably, he never failed to get sufficient money for a fix through stealing, or borrowing, or conniving. He found his Humphrey Bogart fantasy was exhilarating. It gave him a purpose in an otherwise empty, drug- and alcohol-ridden life. His ego was sustained by the fantasy. His images of outsmarting and outmaneuvering people were the strongest influence in his life. It was through these self-images that he saw himself and communicated with himself.

You are probably familiar with James Thurber's character, Walter Mitty. He lived his life the way others defined him—meek, compliant, nonaggressive, and nonassertive. But his secret self-image was of a man who was cool, competent, in control of himself and his destiny in any circumstances. Had Mitty really believed in that secret self-image, he would not have lived a life of "quiet desperation." He would have defied the wife, the boss, and the rest of the people who saw him as a weakling. He would have lived more in congruence with his denied self.

Have you ever observed a person who talks loudly to himself in public? He may be the subject of ridicule. He may be a very disturbed person. However, the people we call normal are also constantly having conversations with themselves, but silently. If we stop to think, we realize that we spend much of our time engaged in reverie, bits of fantasy thoughts, images, ruminations about the past, and dreams of the future. In short, we talk to ourselves through our images as well as our thoughts.

Through our inner conversations, we are constantly assessing our self-image. Sometimes past hurts are re-examined, and felt again. Anticipated fears and joys are rehearsed, sometimes over and over. How do others see us and define us? How are we defining ourselves? Much of our inner conversation deals with the way we make a difference to others, and they to us, and with the kind of self-image confirmation we want from others.

The themes and styles that are characteristic of a person's imagery appear to correlate directly with that person's appraisal of himself.

Your self-esteem is a basic component of your self-image. Your positive and negative attitudes and emotional responses to yourself are polarized aspects of self-esteem. Your competence in all of your endeavors is affected by your level of self-esteem. If you feel unworthy, if you are guilt-ridden, if you have trouble accepting yourself as you are, your self-esteem is eroded and you may fail to realize your full potentialities. As is true in all aspects of self-image, your self-esteem is a composite of your own feelings about yourself and of the feelings others have about you.

Here is an Imaginary Situation which may help you to see how your self-image (and others' perceptions of you) may have changed.

Imagine a series of photographs of yourself. Start as a baby, and then imagine a picture of you at five years of age, then at ten, at twenty, and at successive ages up to the present.

What startling changes do you see in yourself? As you grew and matured physically and intellectually, your self-image must have changed several times. Can you see in this time sequence changes in your parents' definition of you? Changes in your friends' definition of you? Are you still the same person you were at ten? What are the changes?

Now try this Imaginary Situation:

Start at ten inches high and grow into your present size.

This is often a very powerful image. Notice how the process of growth and change reveals different aspects of yourself.

These last two images generally increase awareness of the development of self-image and clarify various aspects of that image. Now try an

Imaginary Situation that will project you into the future.

Imagine that you are staring into a mirror. You see yourself at your present age. Now use your imagination to visualize yourself five years from today. Notice what you see, feel, and do.

Then go another five years into the future. Mentally record your image and what you do, see, and feel. Continue visualizing yourself at five-year intervals and noting your feelings.

I would bet that this image causes strong reactions in you. It almost certainly will have a great deal of meaning to you. Since we are all concerned about how and where we will be in five, ten, or more years from now, this image can give you a picture of the future and your fears and hopes about it. Will you still be doing what you are doing today? Will you make significant changes? Do you like what you see? If not, what will you do to change so that your future will be different?

Nearly all theoretical concepts of therapy emphasize the self-image. Certainly any therapeutic change involves a change in a person's self-image.

The late psychologist Augusta Slesinger developed a concentration technique to increase the possibility of free associations. Part of her method was to ask a patient to think of nothing and to imagine a white movie screen with no pictures on it. After a period of concentration, she would ask the person to get a picture of "I, myself." Her patients sometimes offered substitute selves.

Try this: You may find yourself intimidated by the blank white screen, but force yourself to get a picture of "I, myself" and see what it can tell you. What do you see?

Facing oneself is not easy for many of us. I knew one man who for a period of ten years had not dared look at himself in a mirror. He avoided any reflections of himself at all times. He was so enmeshed in shame and self-hatred that he could not face himself.

Here is a verbatim report from a man who had difficulty seeing his own face.

> During most of therapy when I was asked to imagine myself in a situation, it was nearly impossible for me to visualize my face. I could always see a body, but the only way I could struggle to see my face was to imagine shaving in the morning and therefore looking at myself in an actual situation.
>
> When asked to see myself in a room, I saw a body sitting at the end of a bed, but to see the face was extremely difficult if not impossible. This caused me a great deal of frustrated feelings at the time.
>
> Recently when asked to imagine myself sitting in my own lap, I was able to do it with great ease. At this moment, I am able to do it. This change startled me at first, and then I felt almost overwhelmed with happiness because I could see myself. It felt like I existed—to myself—and that seemed to mean more to me than existing to someone else.

Here is another exercise to use to see your self-image:

Imagine you are looking through a keyhole and you see yourself.

What are you doing in there?
How do you feel?
How do you feel watching the other you?

Are you surprised by this image? It has a strong effect on some people. It may possibly allow you to see certain secret aspects of yourself.

The next image will require concentration. It will give you an in-depth view of your self-image.

Imagine you are looking at yourself looking at yourself.

That's right. It is not a misprint—looking at yourself looking at yourself. There are three positions in this image: the central you, the first observer, and the second observer.

What do you see first?
How does the central you appear to the first observer?
What does the second observer see overall?
How close or far are all three positions in relation to each other?

In this imagery you may very well begin to sense how you look and feel to yourself—that is, the physical and emotional self-image. You may like what you see, or you may not.

Have the first observer make a statement to the central you.
Now imagine a statement from the central you back to the first observer.
Now imagine a dialogue between them.

If you are truly lending yourself to this imagery, you are going to see some of the meaning of your feelings and images. Most of all, you are probably getting to recognize your real self-image.

No two people look at themselves in exactly the same way, so that the reactions to this imaginary situation are various—unique to each person. In some instances, the first self (or the one that is being observed by the second self) may be the one that is deeply involved with a host of conflicts and negative feelings. At other times, the second self may be the target person involved in conflict and bad feelings. The third self, or overall observer, generally does not have the same severity of adverse reactions, but his or her position in the triple-header opens up perspectives of new awareness. One man, Edward, in response to this imaginary situation, gave this sequence:

The first you—The first Edward is well dressed, articulate, sincere, from a good family. He is hollow. He wears a mask. His body is taut—eyes not focusing.

The second you—The second Edward is defiant, insecure, lonely, angry, hostile, with sarcastic humor.

The third you—The third Edward is ground on earth—follows his own intuition and feelings.

> The first me is all the levels of expectation demanded of me. "Be this, Edward; be that, Edward." I don't like the first me, but I don't say to everyone, "I don't want to be him." But I slip into my Edward Two and remain defiant and sarcastic. I operate mainly there. When I go to gatherings of my family, I feel I am supposed to

> go as Edward the First (he laughs) and I play the role, but I secretly operate from Edward the Second and defiance. It's Edward the Third I really want to be because that would be rooted in my own standards and I can give up secretly defying the world.

The self-image is revealed by this situation to have many aspects. It is composed of all the conscious and unconscious attitudes and beliefs we have about ourselves. Because the self-image is so complex and multi-faceted, it can occur to us in many forms.

There is a phenomenon called "Doppelgänger" or "autoscopy," a visual hallucination in which the other person is recognized as being oneself. Usually the Doppelgänger apparition appears without warning and takes the form of a mirror image of the viewer, facing him and just beyond arm's reach. It is life-sized, but very often only the face or head are seen. Generally the image is transparent. A few cases have been reported where a person's double followed him around permanently, like a shadow. Experiences reported by normal people involve isolated episodes of short duration, which occurred during times of stress or fatigue.

The concept of the phantom "double" has perturbed humankind since ancient times. It appears in folklore and fairy stories throughout the world and is prevalent in the religious beliefs of many primitive societies. Shamans and witches cultivate and control their doubles. The shaman double may be dispatched to round up the erring spirit of the patient, or to bring back news of events in far-off places. Some Australian aborigines believe that a man's soul leaves his body after his death and then joins the double in the ancestral cave. The appearance of one's double is common when death is in sight. It is only a small step to presume the double is a harbinger of doom. There is an old German folk belief that Doppelgänger is a sign of imminent death.

The idea of meeting one's double has had a morbid fascination for many creative artists. The list of distinguished writers who have described autoscopic phenomena in this way includes Guy de Maupassant, Oscar Wilde, Franz Kafka, Edgar Allan Poe, John Steinbeck, and Feodor Dostoevsky.

Goethe, a very stable personality, once met himself on the road riding a horse. Shelley, considered to be a much less-balanced person, was walking near the leaning tower of Pisa when he was approached by a figure in a long cloak whose face was concealed by a hood. The figure advanced to within a few feet of the poet before raising the hood. Shelley was terrified to find that it was himself. "Are you satisfied? (Siete sodisfatto?)" inquired his double.

The self-image comes to us in an infinite variety of forms, and the Doppelgänger is one of the most unusual. There is a long history of the mystical nature of seeing one's double. It is not considered to be as common today as it once was—or else we just don't seem to talk about it as freely as our ancestors did.

I am closing this chapter with a segment from *The Seeker*, a novel by Alan Wheelis, which illustrates the power of the self-image in directing our actions and interactions with others. It also shows how intricately our self-image is tied to the image that others have of us.

> We had created for each other an illusion, and by our presence gave it reality for a while. We fell in love, not with each other, but with the image of himself in the other's eyes. These reflections acted and reacted back and forth, cumulatively, and so expanded a nucleus of genuine affection into an illusion of overwhelming passion. At the file cabinet I saw something of eloquence and beauty in her face, and that was the real foundation upon which we built a fairy castle. For in that moment she happened to see my perception of her, found this image of herself pleasing, and began to think more highly of me for my discernment. My next perception discovered in her, therefore, not only the beauty already noticed, but her complimentary appraisal of me; whereupon I realized she must be a woman of extraordinary sensitivity. And when next she glanced at me she noticed this added element in my perception of her which led her again to revise upward her image of me. . . . But she had looked, not into my heart, but into the mirror of my eyes and had seen there only an embellished image of herself. . . . So, I must conclude that what had so enchanted me about her was her appreciation of me. We were strangers looking into each other's eyes and *seeing only ourselves.* (Italics mine.)

In this chapter we have examined self-images, our self-definition. In the previous chapter on

Dual Imagery, we explored the new awareness of conflicts through imagery. In the next chapter, you will explore your body imagery and what it can reveal to you.

CHAPTER V

In What Part of Your Body Does Your Mother Reside?

"What you see is what you get" is a Flip Wilson funny. But what seems even funnier is that nearly all of us, when we look in a mirror, have an inaccurate image of our body. I refer to the perception of ourselves in a mirror and not to the image of our body we would have with our eyes closed.

Alma Cunningham of the Fashion Group, an organization of executive women in the fashion industry, says that we all commonly distort our perceptual mirror image. She discovered this fact while studying proportions of the body to determine the most flattering skirt lengths. Women, asked to describe themselves, consistently misjudged their proportions even while looking in a mirror. Even those women professionally involved with fashion, and concerned daily with such crucial issues as hemlines, couldn't tell whether they had short torsos and long legs or long torsos and short legs. They could look at a model and dress her quite well, but when judging the proportions of their own bodies, they seemed to see themselves according to a preset mental image. One designer kept saying, "My stomach sticks out." She had the flattest stomach in the group.

To prove her point, Ms. Cunningham conducted an experiment at Simplicity Patterns where she works. She put brown paper on a wall and then drew an outline of each of the women involved in creating the patterns. The silhouettes were cut out and mixed up. Then the women were asked to identify them. Not a single woman recognized her own silhouette, including Ms. Cunningham!

Jean Nidetch, president of Weight Watchers, found distortions of body image among fat men. When asked to describe himself, almost every man pictured himself as he had looked when he was graduated from college: broad shoulders; narrow, tapered waist; small hips. Often the men would qualify by saying, "Well, of course my chest is a little bit heavier now," when it was a big, fat belly.

All of us tend to look at our body image through the eyes of others so that what we see in a mirror is interpreted through a set of social values. We evaluate ourselves against an ideal or preferred standard. Thin women, on the whole, like themselves better than fat women, reflecting our cultural bias. In a study done with U. S. Navy men the researchers found that, for men, height was an important factor in self-evaluation. Short men, whether underweight or overweight, had the most unfavorable self-images. Tall, thin men also held themselves in low esteem. Again a cultural bias.

The great Russian writer, Tolstoy, in a book called *Childhood*, said, "I am convinced that nothing has so marked an influence on the direction of a man's mind as his appearance . . . and not his appearance itself so much as his conviction that it is attractive or unattractive."

None of us can escape our body, and the attitudes we have toward it intrude in nearly all our actions. Freud once said that "the ego is first and foremost a bodily ego."

Here is an imagery exercise that may tell you something new about your body and your attitude toward other people.

Imagine the distance you prefer people to stay away from you in ordinary situations. Do not think of someone you are intimately involved with.

Now draw an imaginary line around you to show how close you will allow others to come toward you comfortably.

You have just imaged your "buffer zone." I prefer to call it "allowable space." Were you aware that the space adjacent to your body is an integral part of your body image?

Now try the same exercise with someone more intimate—a relative or a loved one. Do you notice significant differences between the allowable closeness of your intimates and of casual acquaintances? There are some people who can express this difference in inches, feet, yards, or even miles.

Your attitude about yourself determines to some extent how close you will let others come to you. If you have a poor self-image or feel unworthy, you will probably keep people at a distance. One of my patients saw me at the actual distance most of the time, but whenever she imagined or discussed something that she felt guilt or shame about, she would say, "You are now a mile away from me."

Of course, your feelings about the person who approaches are also an important factor in determining the allowable space between you. Usually those you care about can come much closer to you.

There are also cultural standards. Edward Hall, an anthropologist, found that Mediterranean people, e.g. Italians, Greeks, and Arabs, stand much closer to one another than do northern Europeans or Americans.

As you can see, your body extends beyond its skin limits. The next time you feel uneasy while standing and talking to someone, check to see if it stems from the fact that the other person is encroaching on your body space.

W. H. Auden, in *The Birth of Architecture*, beautifully expresses the need for personal space:

> Some thirty inches from my nose
> The frontier of my Person goes,
> And all the untilled air between
> Is private *pagus* or demesne.
> Stranger, unless with bedroom eyes
> I beckon you to fraternize,
> Beware of rudely crossing it:
> I have no gun, but I can spit.

Another important aspect of the body image which is oftentimes overlooked is the concept of self-touching. All of us touch ourselves a lot in the course of a day. We are usually not conscious of our actions. Because of the taboo against talking to oneself, touching becomes one of the few acceptable forms of action in which a person responds directly to himself. It becomes significant because, in a sense, it is an overt representation of an individual's "transactions" with himself.

There is a strong tendency in all of us to inhibit self-touching if we think others are watching us. Try the following images with the idea in mind that you are *not* being observed:

Imagine an image of yourself from head to toe. Which is the easiest part of your body to touch? Imagine touching that part.

Which is the most difficult part to touch? Imagine touching that part.

Does this self-touching image have meaning for you? Some people have difficulty touching those body parts that are considered to be private and not usually talked about. Others experience little or no hesitation in touching any part. My guess is that nearly all of us will have some body parts we touch with some difficulty. The important point is the meaning you attach to each part.

Here is another body image:

Sensing yourself from your head to your toes, what is the body-part core of your identity?

Take your time and select the part you feel is really your core. How do you feel about that part? How do you feel about centering your identity there? Why did you select that particular part?

Here is one man's response to the body-part-core image:

Shorr: Using imagery, in what part of your body is the core of your identity?

Marvin: My core at this moment would be in the back of my neck, probably because I'm most aware of that part of my body. Most of the time during the day I sense that all my tension will go there. I can get tremendous tension all across the neck and shoulders, or I can feel very relaxed there.

Shorr: Why is that particular part of your body the core? Why there rather than anywhere else?

Marvin: Because it's the only part of my body that I'm mostly directly aware of. The minute you asked the question, my mind's eye was there.

Shorr: That's where it was centered?

Marvin: That's right.

Now that you have located the body-part core of your identity you can use it in other imagery exercises.

Imagine your body-part core reacting to other parts of your body. (For example, if you have chosen your heart as the body-part core of your identity, have it say something to your head, your guts, your genitals.) Have the other parts say something back to the core.

Intrabody conversation is quite revealing, leading to awareness of conflict and, often, a lot of surprises. You may be happy or unhappy with some of the interactions.

Let us go further with your body-part core.

Imagine holding your body-part core in your two hands. Who would be the easiest person you know to hand it to? Imagine handing your body-part core to that person.

Check out your feelings as you hand over your core. Why did you select the person you did? What did you imagine that person did with it? What did you imagine that person saying to it? Did it reply?

Now do the same image, but select the person it would be most *difficult* to hand your body-part core to. How did that make you feel? Were you able to do it? Why did you select that person and what kind of reaction did you get? Was there a dialogue?

Spend as much time as you can with this situation. Learn as much as you can about the body part you selected as the core of your identity and why. Ask yourself if you are satisfied or whether you would like to change to a different body part. Learn what you can from the selections of the persons easiest and most difficult to hand your core to. There is a wealth of knowledge about you and your relationships in this sequence.

Any part of the body may be selected as the identity core—your head, face, stomach, genitals, limbs. The image is meaningful when you find out why it is centered in the part you selected. One person said, "It's my heart and it's full of love." Another explained that her identity was in her hands "because I am only what I do."

All parts of the body are important, but there are special implications about our hands. Because they are on the periphery of the body, and because they are so well developed and functional, they are the body part that makes the most significant contact with the rest of the world. We use them to explore inanimate objects, to control the environment, and to accomplish various tasks. We also use them with other people, familiar or strange. We shake hands, extend a helping hand, hold hands, touch and feel others.

Try this imaginary situation by actually using your hands:

Close your eyes and imagine extending both hands out in front of you. Now imagine holding a different person with each hand.

This image often produces very strong feelings. Stay with it for a long enough time to get a clear picture of whom you are holding and how you feel about them. Whom did you grasp with the left hand? Who took your right hand? Were they people you have strong connections to? (People doing this image usually take the hand of a person very close to them. At times they are holding someone they have not seen or thought about for a long time.)

Here is an entirely different use of the hands in imagery:

Imagine a finger that is pointing at you. To what part of your body is it pointing?

Who is pointing the finger? Why is it pointing to that part of your body? You may find that it is an accusing finger. However, it may be pointing to a part of you that you consider a problem area for some reason. You may find other possibilities for interpretation.

The next image moves to a different body part.

Imagine entering your own head. Take your time and allow your imagery to flow. Where do you enter? Where do you go and what do you do and see? Pay attention to your feelings both as the you entering your head and as the you whose head is entered.

Your head is the body part that is related to your thoughts and ideas. This image can show how your mind functions, or perhaps reveal confusion. What part of your head were you most aware of? Your brain? Your ears? Your eyes? Your mouth? Sometimes people go behind their own eyes and look out to get a different perspective of the world.

Check out your feelings about your head. How do those feelings compare to the ones you have about other parts of your body? How do they compare to how you feel about your body as a whole? Early lessons learned from your parents or from religious sources may have restricted awareness and appreciation of your body. You may assume that the only good part of the body is the head. If this is so, have you consistently denied other parts of your body? Are you content to continue in the same way?

We now move to still another area of the body.

Imagine your back and your chest. What is the meaning of these images to you? Now have your chest image say something to your back image. Have your back image say something to your chest image.

Which seems more vulnerable? My experience indicates that the image of the back tends to be more vulnerable that the chest image. Look for the outstanding difference between the two to help you get further meaning from this exercise.

Here is an imaginary situation which uses your whole body:

Imagine lying asleep in a field over night and waking up with footprints on your body.

What part of your body are they on? Why are they on that particular body part? How do you feel about them? Whose footprints are they?

It is possible that whoever you identify as stepping on you is a significant person or force in your life with whom you may be in conflict. How you react to the action and what you do about it may well tell you how you react to that person or force and to that conflict.

Sometimes the footprints belong to an animal or a monster. Look for the meaning implied by your choice of animal or whatever walked on you.

The attitude you have toward your body involves all aspects of your life. Your body is something from which you cannot escape. You adopt attitudes about body size, strength, attractiveness, sexual potency, cleanliness, agility, masculinity, femininity, vulnerability to outside influences, etc. Such attitudes pervade your life decisions. Your body is synonymous with your existence.

We learn early in life to trust body experience as a guide in decision-making. Our size, our strength, our speed and agility determine whether we can cross the street before the oncoming traffic reaches us, whether we can climb a hill, whether we can lift a load. Body experience continues to play an important role throughout life via an elaborate system based on the maze of meanings attached to body areas and the monitoring of sensations from those areas.

For some people, body consciousness leads to hypochondria. Even when a reliable physician assures them that their bodies are intact, they continue to believe in their symptoms and to experience them. Their world is centered in their bodies; all of their fears and anxieties are expressed in body metaphors. Their sense of fragility and inferiority is so profound that they must convince themselves and others that "There is something wrong with my body."

We are still not sure of all the factors contributing to hypochondria, but it may well be that parental attitudes tend to develop the sense of body depreciation.

Seymour Fisher, an authority on body consciousness, in his book, *Body Experiences in Fantasy and Behavior*, explains how parents learn to influence their children in social interactions by directly and indirectly intensifying their awareness of particular body landmarks. A mother focuses an unusual amount of attention (as indicated by the direction of her gaze) upon the lower rear of the child when she wants it to learn anal-sphincter control. She gazes disapprovingly at the eyes of her child when she thinks it is talking too much or being greedy. She finds she can, with such maneuvers, achieve a certain amount of control which does not require a word of explanation. In turn, she may reciprocate by responding to the attention the child focuses on certain areas of her body. The child who feels mother is being too possessive may accusingly direct his gaze to her eyes and produce changes in her behavior. Thus a repertoire of nonverbal strategies, based on calling the other person's attention to some part of the body, can develop in a family. Obviously, a shared concept of the "meaning" of certain body areas would be implicit in such influencing procedures.

It takes years before a child learns to make judgments which are not based on introjected standards, which are given by parents and which are relatively independent of the child's body feelings. So thoroughly are the lessons of childhood learned that a child has difficulty separating his feelings from the attitudes impressed upon him by his parents. His reactions to tabooed and sensitive areas are sometimes retained throughout life. Even if he has consciously overcome them, they may return in times of crisis just as certain kinds of movements are reverted to in emergencies.

Although we all prefer to think of our bodies as our own, in a certain sense we are all "possessed." The way we use our bodies and the attitudes we have about them are not entirely our own; they are the product of our early years of learning and training.

I have found it therapeutically valuable to deal with the concept of possession. In the waking state, which is our major concern, it is "lucid possession." In typical lucid, waking-state possession, the "possessor" is felt to be a hostile intruder like an evil spirit. As such, it has to be banished, cast out from its confines. The same is true if it is derived from an introjected parental figure—a tyrannical father or a witch mother.

Throughout history there have been countless incidents of possession. The accompanying statements and accusations are almost always related to the body of the possessed. It is as if the person no longer owned his own body—or parts of his body. Some outside force—the other—had taken over.

Generally this type of behavior has been associated with persons considered bizarre. The statement "He is possessed by demons" implied that irrational forces had taken him over.

We rarely associate so-called normal persons with such possession. Yet, my experience with hundreds of people has been that it is rather common for them to "sense" or "feel" parts of their body (or all of it) as belonging to parental figures. When a person feels little or no identity of his own, or operates from a false position, he may make bodily identification with a strong parental figure and incorporate that parent "internally."

R. Seidenberg, in an article in *Existential Psychiatry*, reports a case of an individual who was completely dominated by his mother and by the feeling that "he was owned by his mother." The patient talked of "a protoplasmic bridge between them."

I use the following approach in dealing with an incorporated parent. Try it.

Imagine your body as a whole. Now see if you can sense in what part of your body your mother (father) resides?

Let yourself go with this image. How do you feel about having your parent within you? Why is he or she in that particular body part?

Most people are not overly surprised by this question and can usually pinpoint the body part which they feel contains the parent. Naturally the responses are infinitely varied and unique since each person is different and experiences his parents in different ways.

One man sensed his father in his feet. As a child he was constantly afraid of being within his father's sphere of vision. Whenever he saw his father, he wanted to run.

A woman I worked with reported feeling her mother in her shoulder and winced as she told me about it. I asked her if she could attempt to remove her mother through imagery and thus remove her mother's influence. Her first imagery involved a series of operations using a knife. I then asked her if she had to use such a painful method, seeming to hurt herself more in the process of removal. She immediately recognized the masochism in her approach and proudly and smilingly said she had changed her imagery and had made her mother drift out of her back. I then asked her to replace the inner areas where her mother had resided with cool spring water. She did this and became extremely relaxed. "It's the first time I've had that pain out of me for as long as I can remember," she said.

In subsequent meetings with her, I noticed that the pain was gone from the area where she had felt her mother. Her mother's influence on her had lessened. She reported feeling looser and more easygoing. In a sense, it was a minor form of exorcism.

I had seen many people remove mothers and fathers from stomachs, guts, sexual parts, throats, heads, and backs. Every part of the body is subject to this form of possession. Invariably, some pain or inner tension is alleviated and changed behavior patterns emerge.

Body symptoms are often a compromise solution for a dilemma or conflict. Such compromises may be a protection against even greater breakdown. If, for example, we have been falsely defined in the formative years and if that definition is different from the way we feel "in our heart of hearts" about ourself, a polarized conflict emerges. The false definition may then take on a bodily form. The mother or father who "resides" in the person's chest—or any other part—is in reality the false identity, or the neurotic conflict internalized. Removing the influence of the "other" from the body part through imagination helps bring about a healthy resolution of conflict.

If in doing this imagery, you find a parent in a body part that is chronically troublesome to you, you may profit by finding a way to remove the possessor. Imagine a way to free yourself from an alien resident. It may take you several tries to finally rid yourself of an unwanted intruder, but the results are certainly worth the effort.

Do not overlook the possibility that you may have incorporated a loved one very comfortably. One young lady felt her grandmother all through her body and was very pleased to have her there. She was also very happy to carry her father in her heart. Her voice was soft and gentle as she spoke of these imaginary inhabitants of her body. There was, however, a marked change in her voice and her expressions as she told of sensing her mother in her chest and lungs. She felt as if there were iron in there. With great effort she was able to image her mother out of her body. She uttered a long sigh of relief when the task was completed.

A thirty-one-year-old patient, whose symptoms included inarticulation and speech hesitancy, responded to this question by saying his mother resided in his vocal chords. Here is a verbatim account of how we "exorcised" her.

Shorr: I want you to imagine you are entering your mother's body.

Bob: . . . my first image was to enter her mouth—but I was afraid I'd be stretching her jaws apart—that's repulsive and ugly, like tearing it apart.

Shorr: Try to enter the mouth anyway.

Bob: I'll try—I'm standing on the back of her tongue, looking around; I slide off the tongue into the vocal chords. It looks like a prison. I am a prisoner of the vocal chords. In fact, I am an enemy of the vocal chords. They should recognize I'm not an enemy. Now they appear more like they are alive, and they are not steel bars. They can move.

Shorr: Pluck the chords as if they were harp strings.
Bob: O.K.–good music–but I'm still a prisoner.
Shorr: How can you define your (her) vocal chords so that they don't define you?
Bob: I can fight back.
Shorr: O.K., fight back.
Bob: (Long pause.) How do you fight back? I am tickling the base of each vocal chord and uncontrollably each one is opening up–so I can get out–I run up the tongue and I jump out of the mouth to freedom.
Shorr: Now how do you feel about your own vocal chords?
Bob: I can define them and then show me how it works. I can say anything I want to, whenever I want to.
Shorr: Keep defining them.
Bob: They are nothing but my servants; they are only mechanisms of sound.
Shorr: Try screaming, "I have the final authority over you."
Bob: I HAVE THE FINAL AUTHORITY OVER YOU. (Continues in normal tone) They are nothing but a bunch of vibrations. They can't think; they will not define me. They are my prisoner.
Shorr: I get the feeling you gave the vocal chords a separate identity.
Bob: It became alive and told me what I can say or what I can't say. Like my mother, "Never say anything wrong to anyone or they will leave you"–that's my conflict.
Shorr: Enter your mother's body again.
Bob: Through the mouth. All I feel is revenge; this is what you did to me. Now I'm going to

show you what it feels like. (Pause) It deprived me of my hostility towards her. I couldn't liberate from her person. I had to be perfect or I could expect the worst.

Earlier I asked you to do an image which showed the body core of your identity. Then you tried finding in which part of your body your parents reside. Let's carry this type of imagery a step farther.

In what part of your body does your anger reside? Take your time and sense your body from your head to your toes, to determine your anger body part.

Now put your hand on that body part and then conjure up what vocal sound would express that anger. As you physically localize it, let the sound out. In short—localize and vocalize.

You will probably reduce the heightened anger associated with that body part as you do the exercise. Are you feeling a sense of relief? Try to find out why your anger is in that specific part. Is it a part of you that was denied by a parent? Is it a part that is weak or not well developed?

Here is a man's response to that image:

Stan: When I feel anger, it generally comes in the pit of my stomach, and not being very body oriented—in terms of being aware of my body—it takes pain to become aware of it and that's why I chose this part. My anger I always feel just below the sternum.

Shorr: What would your anger say to me?

Stan: I have trouble with that because my anger isn't there now. It comes from distrust or feeling someone's not respecting me—giving me full measure. I don't feel any anger right now to you, but you know that I would see to it that your therapy would not work—I would prove at all costs that it would not work on me. That was probably the most subtle anger that I would experience.

Shorr: It sounds like defiance.

Stan: Defiance, but it's—I can recall many occasions when I would feel twinges of it when I felt I was getting close to something—if I felt *you* were.

Shorr: Then you would defy me by denying whatever was brought up?

Stan: Right—thereby defeating myself.

Shorr: So your anger really is a kind of defiance?

Stan: Toward you—a subtle thing—toward other people. I'm aware of it toward other people. I'm definitely aware of it now on much less subtle levels, and I definitely feel it in my stomach.

One very fat lady, when asked where her anger resides, poked a finger into the rolls of flesh around her middle and said, "In here. And when I am angry, I eat and eat." She buried her anger under all the fat and drowned her feelings by eating.

Besides anger, there is joy, love, or even inner energy within the body. With each of these emotions, you can ask the same question: In what part of your body does your joy, or love, or energy reside? Each is a valuable clue to self-awareness. As you progress you will find it ever easier to understand the messages your body is constantly giving you.

Body imagery can be quite dramatic when we are dealing with aches and pains. For example, do you have a pain in your back, or your neck, or some other spot?

Imagine entering your own body and traveling to the spot that gives you pain. Take your time as you travel. When you arrive at your pain point, look at the spot and imagine pouring some warm, soothing oil on the spot. It probably feels better as you imagine the warm liquid on it.

Relief of pain gained in this manner is probably due to alleviation of tension. As a child you centralized pain and tension in specific parts of your body. Perhaps some were the result of imitation of one parent or the other as they put their hands to their head or chest—or whatever part—and expressed pain or tension verbally or through groans. You probably picked up their gestures and used them unconsciously for the same feelings.

In the past few years we have become more attuned to body language, and there is a growing body of scientific knowledge about how we use our bodies to make statements and to convey messages nonverbally. Shakespeare recognized this fact four hundred years ago and stated it beautifully in *Troilus and Cressida*:

> There's a language in her eye, her cheek, her lip—
> Nay her foot speaks, her wanton spirits look out
> At every joint and motive of her body.

Up until now you have been imaging your own body. You can learn as much by imaging the bodies of others both separately and in interaction with you.

Image again the body-part core of your identity. Now say something from that body-part core to a person you know. It can be anyone you choose. Then have that person say something back to your body-part core.

Now imagine the body-part core of the other person. When you have done that, try to have a core-to-core dialogue.

What has been revealed by this image? Pay attention to the meaning of the body part you see as that other person's identity core. You may even want to check with the other to see if you both agree on the body-part core of each. Certainly you will begin to understand some of the underlying motives in the relationship even if the core-to-core dialogue does not go beyond your imagination.

Still another powerful imagery involves the process of staring at another person in imagination.

You are to imagine staring at the naked back of your father. Tell yourself what you see, feel, and do.

Stay with this image for several minutes. What strong feelings are released by this image? Now reverse the imagery and have your father stare at your naked back. Do you find old binds? Good feelings? Forgotten reminiscences?

The identical imagery can be done with your mother as well as with any other significant person in your life. The reversal of positions between you and the other person intensifies and clarifies the feelings this image conjures up.

Now carry this imaginary situation a step further:

Imagine entering the body of your father (mother). Imagine each parent entering your body.

Spend time really exploring the other body. Travel around, noting carefully what you see, feel, and do.

One of my patients gave the following account of such an imagined journey.

> I enter my father's body through his stomach. His stomach is thickly congested with fog. Blindly feeling my way through the fog, I find a safe-deposit box. Inside, it is filled with cobwebs. At the bottom of this box lies my father's heart. What a terrifying sight! His heart is dark brown and it's dead. I can't stand to look at it. It's revolting! It's morbid! It's rotten! I say to his heart, "All of my life I have been most curious to know what you are all about. I've always felt that there was something much deeper about yourself that you have never exposed. Now I am looking at it before my eyes. Only a man with a dead heart would have to live off the lives of others. And only a man with a dead heart would use his daughter for his own means, and at the same time try to suffocate me from my own sense of self. Inducing in me what you couldn't accept in

yourself—that you are the rotten person, not me." Of course, my father's heart could not reply, it's dead.

My father enters my body through my guts. He feels threatened and frightened by the echoes of truth that the depths of my guts reveal. My guts are echoing to him that I am not what he has tried to make me. I will not accept responsibility for his own rottenness. My father cannot bear the pain that it brings him, so he violently fights back with sudden anger as he intellectually and physically makes every effort to degenerate me with his own degeneracy. When he finds my heart, he is overwhelmed by its intensity. It is bright red, healthy, and well endowed with warmth, human depth, and a great eagerness to live. My father's reaction to my heart is disapproval. He cannot afford to accept it. If he accepts my heart, then he has to accept his own rottenness. I don't feel that my father could say anything to my heart. He would merely deny it.

This image brought forth very deep feelings. The twenty-four-year-old woman who experienced it was not ordinarily articulate, but she was able to express herself clearly while doing this image. The feelings were so strong, she had no difficulty in describing them.

You can do this image using any other significant person in your life. You can imagine your journey through the other's body and then the reverse. However, you may benefit even more if the other person is present and can make the journey through your body in his own imagination.

Mutual body travel is a useful exercise for increased understanding between two persons who are emotionally involved. Try this with a loved one.

Each person imagines entering the other's body. Notice where you enter, where you go, what you do, what you see and feel. Then each in turn shares the experience verbally with the other.

There are numerous surprises in store for adventurous travelers. As the one taking the journey, you can get in touch with your true feelings and your image of your partner. You become more aware of those parts of the body that attract or repel you. You find hidden emotions becoming apparent. This is the way to bring both positive and negative feelings to light and to share them.

When you hear the account of the voyage through your body, you are able to see your image through the eyes of your loved one. You may be delighted to find that you are held in greater esteem than you had thought. You may find that a part of you that you don't particularly like is especially endearing to the other. On the other hand, this is a chance to learn what parts of your body, or of your behavior, turn your partner off or are irritating.

In group situations when I have asked people to journey through someone's body, I have heard some astounding replies. People enter through the eyes, the mouth, the navel, the vagina, the pores. Once inside they find computers, pools of tears; soft, velvety pinkness; circular staircases; dark caverns; libraries; three-ring circuses. At times it has brought people very close to one another, and at other times it has released repressed hostility and anger. If one person has difficulty entering another's body—or refuses altogether—there is usually undetected or unexpressed anger or distaste which becomes rapidly evident.

I often suggest the use of body parts communicating with the same body parts of another to get at the reality of interpersonal relationships. For example:

Imagine what your head would say to your mother's head.

Imagine what your heart would say to your mother's heart.

Imagine what your guts would say to your mother's guts.

Imagine what your penis (vagina) would say to your mother's vagina.

Imagine what each part of your mother would say to the same part of you.

Naturally, you can do this image using your father's body parts as well. You can also do it with your loved one, with your children, or anyone else you choose. Also, there are numerous variations on this imaginary situation, and you will find it increasingly meaningful as you add successive statements to the dialogue.

Imagine what your head would say to your mother's heart.

Imagine what your head would say to your mother's guts.

Imagine what your head would say to your mother's vagina.

Imagine what each part of your mother would say to your head.

Your heart can speak to each part, your guts can speak to each part, and your penis (vagina) can speak to each part. Each interaction and each additional line of dialogue adds another dimension to the growing understanding of the many interwoven threads that make up the fabric of a relationship.

The following is an example of the way a young woman responded (in part) to this form of imaginary situation—an interaction between her body parts and those of her parents:

1. My head would say to my mother's head: "I'm strong and I know how to compete with men on their terms. I won't be weak like you."
2. Heart to heart: "Look at yourself, Mom. Become your whole self. Don't allow everyone to destroy your heart."
3. Guts to guts: "Don't play martyr with me. Give up trying to manipulate me. I'm tired of it."
4. Vagina to vagina: "I'm alive and healthy and like to be sexual. It's great!"

1. My mother's head to mine: "Straighten up; think of what people say; think of your reputation. Go to school."
2. Her heart to mine: "I need you; I love you; I am afraid for you. Let me and your father protect you."

3. Her guts to mine "You must be cautious; the world is a frightening place; be afraid."
4. Her vagina to mine: "We are prisoners. This is the only part of a woman men like; watch out for them."

1. My head to my father's head: "I can compete with you and do well. I am as good as you."
2. My heart to his heart: "What are you doing? Are you crazy? You are hurting everyone you love. Stop it!"
3. My guts to his guts: "I'm not afraid of you anymore."
4. My vagina to his penis: "Stay away from me! Learn to love your wife."

1. His head to mine: "You are sharp but need a lot of refining. Learn from me how to talk logically and be able to get your point across."
2. His heart to my heart: "Be careful; don't get hurt. I can't stand to see you hurt, because then I hurt too."
3. His guts to mine: "Enjoy life; do all you can; learn all you can. Don't be like your mother."
4. His penis to my vagina: It would say nothing overtly, but subtly indicate that it was there, just there, not going to do anything, but be omnipresent.

It should become clear to you how this image, as it is continued, will add to your understanding of your feelings about others and how you perceive them reacting to you.

The next imaginary situation has two parts. You are to do them separately.

1. Imagine taking a shower with your mother. What do you do? How do you feel? What does your mother do?

2. Imagine taking a shower with your father. What do you do? How do you feel? What does your father do?

Reflect on what body parts are referred to in the images and the feelings about those parts. Notice which parts are avoided or ignored. You may begin to understand how you developed some of your attitudes about your body and the bodies of others. You will probably discover some unexpressed feelings about your parents. They can be either positive or negative feelings.

Do the next imaginary situation in the same way—first with one parent and then, separately, with the other.

Imagine your mother (father) on your back. How do you feel? What do you do? What does she (he) do?

Do you like the feeling of one or the other parent on your back? Is it a burden? Are you angry? Helpful? Weighed down? Cheerful? What are you going to do about it? If you are angry, burdened, resentful, imagine how you would go about removing your parent from your back. How does that makes you feel?

Here is an imagery sequence that can reveal more than just your feelings about your parents.

Imagine that you, your mother, and your father are all lying nude in bed. What happens? How do you feel? What do you say to one another?

This image may lead to possible confrontations with one or both of your parents about denied body parts. It may help explain your attitudes about touching, about odors, about nudity. Here is the response of an older woman to this imaginary situation.

> I immediately flashed back to the apartment we lived in when I was in my early teens. That would make my mother about thirty-five and my dad about forty. She was in one of her heavy periods. She must have been fifteen or twenty pounds overweight, with big thighs and hips. My dad was big—six feet two inches and over two hundred pounds.
>
> It is daylight—probably morning—and I am lying stiff and uncomfortable on the very far edge of the mattress. It is hard to imagine my parents nude and even harder to imagine myself nude with them. It is a regular double bed because they didn't have king-size beds in those days.
>
> My dad is in the middle and my mother is on the other side. I am lying on my side facing away from them. My parents are lying on their backs. We are all carefully covered by the blankets. They are lying apart and talking over family matters while I just lie there listening, wondering why I am there. There is no physical contact between any two of us. We don't even look at each other. I would like to snuggle up to my dad the way I did when I was a little girl, but I know my

mother would misconstrue. Also, it would probably embarrass my dad because I was well developed by thirteen. All feelings are as carefully concealed as our bodies.

I feel miserable and superfluous, so I slip very quietly out of the bed, quickly throw on a robe and leave the room without looking at my parents. They continue to talk for a while and then they, too, get up and start the day.

This brings back a lot of unpleasant feelings for me. We never made a big thing about nudity or privacy. No one paraded around undressed, but we had to share one bathroom so the door was seldom locked and anyone might enter. I also had to share a bedroom with my brother until I was about eighteen. He was seven years younger. We had a tacit agreement to maintain a semblance of privacy. Also our hours for rising and retiring were different. But I missed some sense of freedom.

At that time I was so unaware of my body I didn't even notice my breasts had developed until someone at school in gym pointed out that I should be wearing a bra. I hated to shower in gym and when it was necessary would try to cover myself completely with a towel. I really wasn't comfortable with my body until many years later and only enjoyed being nude when I knew I was alone. I developed round shoulders and very bad posture because I tried for so many years to conceal my breasts.

Now I am much more comfortable with my body, but I still dislike it a lot because I am overweight and look a lot like my mother did in those days. Apparently I don't dislike it enough to lose the extra twenty pounds I carry. At least I am able to accept it and to reveal it in the proper circumstances.

Body imagery can tell us a lot about our personality and about attitudes toward our bodies. It also gives valuable clues and meanings about our sexual identity, core experiences, and a myriad of self-attitudes. Body imagery is a complex subject. In this chapter we have attempted to get a broader view of this vast area.

CHAPTER VI

X-Rated Images

You can fantasize or imagine sexual happenings from memory images almost as if you were actually experiencing them. On occasion, sexual imageries are so vivid that the physiological response is the same as that in intercourse. There is an increase in the heartbeat rate, a rise in temperature, rapid breathing, vasocongestion, and even orgasm. Of course, other images besides sexual ones can be recreated this way, but sexual images are certainly the vivid example par excellence.

When people tell me they never have images, I ask them to imagine sexual scenes or recall sexual memories. So far this has resulted in no failures. I remember Rick, a thirty-five-year-old man, who said he could not really image anything. Yet he had no trouble reporting with great vividness and excitement an image of himself as a voyeur watching two lesbian women engaged in sexual contact.

Sexual themes are a fertile area for the human imagination. They have power because of their importance in our lives. Actual images of sexual contact are but one kind of conjured imagery. These are the images we have during sex acts, or in place of the act. There are other images related to the strategies of interaction between men and women that anticipate sexual outcomes.

Surprisingly, we do not yet know exactly what creates sexual excitement. We do know that the sources are not purely physiological. Imagery plays a vital role—it is, in fact, essential. Subjective reports of erotic fantasies and daydreams show us that certain themes recur frequently. The sexual images that we respond to are, perhaps, unique to each individual, yet there are common factors. As yet no scientific studies have been completed that can explain why the images that "turn on" some people fail to "turn on" others.

Excitement, in general, comes from dealing with the unknown—the mysteries of life. It stems also from facing risks. These may be real or imagined threats of mistreatment or danger. They may be the risks involved in expressing hostility we feel toward others who have more power than we do.

The same elements of risk are also a sexual stimulus at times. There is an excitement in danger, and in our fantasies we can select risks which have a possibility of a successful outcome. We can do things in fantasy we would never dream of actually doing. We are excited by running controlled risks.

It seems that hostility, too, plays a part in sexual fantasy. Psychologists do not understand fully why hostility should be a sexual stimulator; nevertheless, it is frequently a component of sexual excitement. In such a case we have the thrill of confronting and besting someone within the safety of our fantasies.

The objects of our fantasies very often become the same people we pick in the real world. However, they are not as manipulable in reality as they can be in imagery, so there is the excitement of having the scenario played out differently from our expectations.

Illusion and mystery also seem to be important elements in sexual excitement. We attempt in various ways to create the illusion of perfection or desirability that will attract others. Familiarity may lead to boredom, but excitement can be generated or heightened by the subtle and tantalizing suggestion of hidden charms and unexplored facets of personality. The childhood mysteries about the opposite sex are carried over into the adult world and we seek constantly to solve them.

In our sexual fantasies we play out the early dramas of our lives which have been instrumental in shaping our attitudes toward sex, toward our bodies, and toward the bodies of the opposite sex. We may use these images to reverse traumas of the past, to experience triumph and revenge. If, as children or young adults, we felt powerless, we can in fantasy restore the balance of power and rehearse the behavior that will help us to develop the sense of self we have been denied. All of this is integrated into our real world, although often unconsciously, and affects what will stimulate us sexually.

Our early relationships with our parents combined with our experiences during adolescence often determine what will later be sexually exciting. The actual experiences vary from person to person, resulting in unique individual responses.

All our countless interactions and ego involvements develop into images. Sadistic or masochistic imagery may emerge, as well as images of dominance, submission, rejection, and acceptance. Unfavorable comparisons, feelings of heartbreak, joy, sin, being dirty are all present. All of these relationships and feelings are possible at one time or another in the sexual interactions of men and women. They are also possible between members of the same sex. Often our imageries reveal not only how we feel about the opposite sex, but also about the members of our own sex.

Try this example of an imaginary situation that can indicate the subtle or obvious byplays between men and women:

Imagine you are escorting a group of prisoners of the opposite sex one mile away to another prison area. Take your time and follow the image to its conclusion.

How did you treat the prisoners?
What did you do?
What did they do?

Now imagine escorting prisoners of the same sex.

The responses to this exercise are quite varied and can indicate the strategies of reacting to the same or the opposite sex. One man imagined freeing the women and becoming sexually involved with all of them. Another man, strictly and by the rules, carried out his assignment with great detail and carefulness. Still another reaction came from a woman, who, in escorting women prisoners, was even harsher and more exacting than the second man.

The interpersonal strategies of coping with men and women can be revealed by such an image. It is but a step further to uncover a person's particular style, defenses, and conflicts.

Try another general tvpe of imagery and report what you see as the images appear:

Imagine looking through a hole in a wall. What do you see?

Were you surprised bv what you saw?
Is there some secret element in your image?

This particular imagery can elicit secret feelings, quite often of a sexual nature (but not always).

Very often there are things related to sex that people cannot, or will not, talk about. There are things that they hide even from themselves. Since sexual conflicts deal with the most vulnerable, the most tender, the most shame-inducing and the most guilty feelings, they are the most difficult to disclose to oneself and to others. In order to get at these conflicts I use general imaginary situations which have no sexual overtones, but which have, through clinical use, proved to be revealing. Doing several of these general images often helps to free a person from some inhibitions so that the more obviously sexual images are not so threatening. Let's proceed by degrees from general imageries to more explicit types.

Here is a general imaging exercise:

Actually put both fists out in front of you and then imagine a different image in each fist.

What images did you get?

Can you compare your images?

Can you interchange them—move them from one hand to the other?

Can you guess what psychological truths the images may reveal?

Here is the report of a man who did that imagery:

> I imagined a different image in each fist. In the right fist was a crystal ball. Inside the crystal ball there was a woman, more specifically a ballerina. In the left fist I imagined a small snake or worm. This object had no apparent significance at the moment, and thus I discarded it. I then turned my attention back to the ballerina, who began to grow and become more lifelike as I concentrated on her. I had ambivalent feelings about her. On the one hand I could touch her and feel her warmth. At that moment she represented the warmth I wanted and needed from other people, especially women. Then she became cold and detached from any feeling. I could no longer touch or feel her. At this point I did not know why I

could not make contact with her, but I felt that the feeling of detachment had occurred because I wanted it to.

Then Joe asked me to imagine the snake or worm in my fist again. It was at this point that the snake's relationship to myself and the ballerina became clear. The snake represents sexual fantasy, a very secretive fantasy. It takes the form of a snake because it is something I am ashamed of and something which I have clearly suppressed looking at for most of my life. Even at this point it is very hard for me to get in touch with the total significance of this imagery. However, I do know that sexual fantasy has always been a source of excitement and meaning in my life. It was, and still is, to some extent, the method I use to compensate for feelings of inferiority. This is especially true in relationship to my own sense of masculinity. Any aggressive step not taken in the world, especially in relation to a woman, was suppressed and covered over by a fantasy. Also sexual fantasy is very safe. That is, there is no way to be "trapped" in a relationship if it isn't real.

The fantasy was and still is, to some extent, something external from me; it's out there almost unachievable, which in effect, makes it exciting. But it, in turn, makes reality, that is, dealing with women, almost of a secondary nature.

At one point in the imagery, Joe asked me to imagine myself as the snake. I did so, and immediately imagined myself wrapped around my own wrist. This is almost a perfect isolation. It is my way of not confronting all the fears I mentioned previously. And it prevents me from experiencing feelings of warmth, love, and sharing to my fullest capacities.

Were you able to get as much out of your imagery? If you did not, perhaps you are holding back. Do you feel apprehensive? Relax and try another general image.

Imagine three doors, and imagine entering each door. Let yourself go and immerse yourself in the images. Record what you see, what you do, and what you feel.

I find from clinical experience that nearly always certain clear patterns emerge. Usually the middle door seems to indicate something about your sexual or romantic relationships with the opposite sex. Before you become confused, let me hasten to explain, however, the image seen in the middle door does not have to be an actual sexual scene or make direct reference to sex. For example, one woman said when she entered the middle door, she saw empty cupboards and it made her sad. When asked if this image had meaning for her, she replied, "Yes, it's very much like my life with men, empty and sad."

There are people who do imagine actual sexuality or love relationships in the middle-door image. Frequently, I have people respond with images of a significant other lying in bed beyond the middle door. They enter the room and react to the person in the image as they would, or would like to, in a real situation. The meaning of the middle-door image is directly related to your own inner or phenomenological world. Therefore, it is up to you to give it meaning.

Obviously no image is absolutely guaranteed every time to yield the same meaning, but the responses to this particular exercise have been sexually related images 98 per cent of the time.

I am sure you are curious about the other doors. Certain characteristic patterns emerge, but they are not as readily discernible as the middle-door image. You may have to do some exploring, but it will be worth it.

One of the two remaining doors will elicit an imagery sequence that will reflect the way you relate in your social and interpersonal life—the outer world of existence. Competitiveness, the need for achievement, the desire for social acceptability, or any other attitude or strategy of dealing with the outside world may reside behind either the first or the third door. My guess is that you will readily detect which it is.

The final door will lead to an imagery that reveals something about your inner self. It may be your deeper self-image or perhaps some aspects of your unconscious.

I do not restrict the use of imagery to work with individuals. In my own work with couples, I have found it interesting and effective to use imagery in examining their relationships. A fruitful approach is to have partners try to predict one another's images. It works like this:

First, each person is asked to imagine five consecutive images silently and to record them. Then each person in turn is asked to guess what images the partner has visualized. Many surprises occur. At times a couple's accuracy in predicting one another's images has the quality of extrasensory perception. There is a high degree of awareness of the inner world of the other. But more often, there is disparity and great separateness of the private visions of the couple. An awareness of this can lead to greater understanding and eventually bring them closer together. Little else unites two people as sharing inner worlds can.

Predictive imagery works equally well with any two people who are connected in some form of relationship. It can be between parent and child, other close relatives, or friends and can help establish greater understanding and help form a stronger bond between them.

There is one imaginary situation that can be extremely effective in fostering awareness of sexual matters. It has the effect of showing where it "really is." Let me introduce it to you.

You are to imagine removing lint from the navel of your partner. You are to relax and allow the free flow of imagery.

What do you see, feel, and do? As you allow yourself to experience this imagery I am sure it will be quite revealing to you.

When you have completed the first part of the imagery, reverse it and imagine your partner removing lint from your navel. Imagine what the partner sees, feels, and does.

Now compare and integrate the two experiences and a great deal of meaningful material may become apparent.

Lovers' strategies in dealing with each other take many forms. Often they seem to be contests. This, of course, carries a connotation of victory and defeat within a relationship. You can test for this quality by using the Finish-the-Sentence technique. Ask your partner to finish these sentences:

It is a victory when I can get you to ________.

It is a defeat when you make me ________.

Now reverse the procedure, and you finish those sentences as they are stated by your partner.

What do you learn about your relationship when you each take a turn finishing the sentence:

I need to deprive you of the satisfaction of ___?

Imagination can run wild in love and in sexual relationships and can conjure visions of slights, rejections, disapproval, or inadequacy. We can anticipate exciting sexual contact in imagination. Often the image of a loved one can sustain a person when long distances or stretches of time are involved.

But it is in jealous reactions that our imagination runs the wildest—where images are a constant source of torture. Imagery can fan the flame of jealousy to the point where it becomes destructive to the relationship and possibly to the well-being or to the life of the concerned individuals.

We have all heard tales of excessive jealousy and the corrosive effects it can have on relationships. Probably the most well-known story is that of Othello and Desdemona. Othello's jealousy takes the form of suspiciousness that denies reason. He distorts, misreads, and misjudges evidence so that "trifles light as air are . . . confirmations strong as proofs of holy writ."

There are numerous counterparts to Othello's story in drama, literature, and the daily newspapers. Ernest Jones, in his book *Jealousy*, once wondered what would be left in French newspapers if they omitted all stories of *crimes passionels.* We are familiar with the theme, but do we realize what important roles are played by imagination and imagery?

A young man who is excessively jealous of his wife is haunted constantly by visions of her with other men. His imagination runs wild. He reads meaning into a smile at the butcher; he imagines her entertaining a strange man at home while he is at work; he is in agony when she is out of sight at a party.

As his images become more vivid, his feelings become stronger. His suspicions grow. Obsessed by his images, he may begin making accusations, trying to trap his wife into an admission of guilt, watching her every move and expression. His images block out reality. Rational thought deserts him. As the inner tensions mount, he may feel the need to release some of the pressure through action.

He telephones at odd hours to see where she is and what she is doing. He follows her. If he can, he may hire a detective to report on her movements. He questions her constantly. All the while, his images torture him with pictures of what he dreads most.

Soon it may be impossible for him to distinguish between images and reality. There we have the seeds of disaster. His constant suspicion and accusations may finally destroy her love and force her to turn away from him—perhaps permanently.

If the relationship continues and he is still possessed and consumed by jealousy, he may resort to violence. His violence may be directed toward his wife, toward the imagined rival, or toward himself. He may assault or even murder.

Tolstoy suggested that there is a premeditative aspect of jealous murder. He points out in his *Kreutzer Sonata* that there was no temporary insanity when Pozdnuishef killed his wife. He was perfectly aware of what he was going to do and was conscious all the time he was committing his crime.

> "When people say that in a fit of fury they do not remember what they are doing," confessed Pozdnuishef, "they are telling an untruth. I remember everything, nor did I stop remembering for a single second. The more I raised within me the steam of my fury, the more clearly did the light of consciousness burn within me so that I could not help seeing all I was doing. I knew every second what I was doing. . . . I know I struck her below the ribs, and that the dagger would enter. At the very moment when I was doing it I knew that I was doing something terrible, something which I had never done before, and which would have terrible consequences. But this consciousness flashed like lightning, and the deed followed immediately after the consciousness."

Jealousy is experienced by both sexes and at all ages. Women experience just as much as men the suspicions, the fears, the exaggerations, the wild images, and the lack of reason that characterize this emotion.

Jealousy is common to all. Only when it goes beyond the point of being a fleeting emotion soon controlled by calm rational thought does it become unusual or dangerous. If one broods about it, becomes obsessed by it, then the images evoked can lash one into a frenzied rage. The primary emotion may be love, but when it is distorted by jealousy, it may turn to revenge.

Erotic fantasies are more than just therapeutic tools used to reveal inner conflicts or the strategies we use in interrelationships. They are intimately related to our innermost nature and fulfill several positive functions.

In a study done by Jerome L. Singer and E. Barbara Hariton, and reported in the *Journal of Consulting and Clinical Psychology*, it was suggested that imaging during sexual intercourse should be considered in the general analysis of feminine psychology and that it is unreasonable to link fantasies to neuroses. They found that women who tend to daydream in other situations were most likely to fantasize during intercourse, and the fantasies served to enhance the experience.

Harry Benjamin and R. E. L. Masters point out the positive function of imagination:

> Ralph Waldo Emerson once said that imagination is not a talent of some men, but is the health of every man. Prostitution thrives on man's capacity for imagination. The endless variety of human sexual stimulants is matched by the endless variety of illusions. The prostitute who is able to create the illusion of an ideal sex partner, fleeting as it may be, has actually done something for this

man's mental health, short-lived and often followed by disillusionment as it may be.

Doctors Phyllis and Eberhard Kronhausen, in *Erotic Fantasies*, also show us that erotic fantasies can operate on several levels and have important bearing on our attitudes and behavior:

> . . . Without knowledge of an individual's sex fantasies, however, any information about his sexual behavior would be one-sided and perhaps totally misleading. A person may, for example, have no actual incidence of homosexual or sadomasochistic acting out in his sex history, and yet his entire fantasy life may revolve around such situations or be tinted by them.
>
> . . . Among persons with colorless personalities one finds some of the most gaudy sex fantasies, though they would be horrified at the mere idea of acting out any part of them in real life.

Nikolai Gogol's biographers reveal him as a lifelong masturbator who probably never had sexual contact with a woman. His masturbatory fantasies were satisfied and were even of assistance in the process of concocting ridiculous adventures for his story "The Nose," in which the detached nose, freed from the rest of its body, followed its wayward inclinations. One journal rejected the story because of its obscenity.

We use our imageries in both positive and negative ways. They can compensate for intolerable life situations, or they can complement and enhance them. They can also mask parts of ourselves that we cannot, or will not, deal with.

See what you learn from this image:

Imagine there are two of you. Then imagine kissing yourself.

Do you recoil from yourself?

Is it difficult to get close or to feel warmth and love for that other you?

Perhaps your self-image is really so bad that it contaminates all of your other relationships.

On the other hand, you may have enjoyed kissing yourself. You may have tremendous self-love. You really are the person you want to be.

But look a little deeper. Is what you feel self-esteem and self-respect? Or have you carried it so far that you love yourself too much to the exclusion of others?

This brings to mind a familiar theme. Perhaps you recall the ancient Greek myth about Narcissus and Echo. Narcissus was so beautiful that all the girls who saw him longed to be his, but he would have none of them. He would pass the loveliest carelessly by, no matter how much she tried to make him look at her. It was the same with Echo, the fairest of the nymphs, who had fallen in love with Narcissus. One day Echo beckoned rapturously to him with her arms outstretched. But Narcissus turned away from her in angry disgust and asserted, "I will die before I give you power over me." Then he was condemned by the goddess Nemesis to fall in love with his own reflection in a pool. "Now I know," he cried, "what others have suffered from me, for I burn with love of my own self—and yet how can I reach that loveliness I see mirrored in the water? But I cannot leave it. Only death can set me free." And so he died, ceaselessly pining after his own mirror image.

Freud used this myth to symbolize the self-absorption and self-infatuation that represent a fixation upon one's own self as a sexual love object. The concept of self-love and its meaning in our relationships with others has been an important aspect of man's development all through history. The myth and other tales with similar themes suggest that the balance between self-love and love of others is a delicate one requiring constant evaluation.

I pointed out earlier our two existential needs, the need to make a difference to someone and the need for acknowledgment or confirmation of our existence. They are equally applicable to the sexual sphere as they are to other areas of life. Here they manifest themselves in two pervasive concepts which underlie the individual's feelings about sexuality. I call these concepts "Allowable Sex" and "If I Can't Make a Difference to Someone."

The need to make a difference to someone is the despairing cry of people whose sexual identity is of such little value that they settle for a counterfeit of the real thing. Usually these individuals have homosexual tendencies, but this is not always the case. One man went with a woman for more than a decade—sharing many extended experiences, yet he was never allowed to engage in actual sexual intercourse. She controlled him. Seething underneath, he nevertheless accepted his denied state. Nobody explains this position better than Laing in *The Self and Others*:

> A man who despairs at his own power to make any difference to a woman may be prepared

therefore to settle for a good counterfeit of the "real" thing, deriving pleasure from the very complexity of the disillusionment and illusionment involved in the play of mutual indifference, meanness and generosity, helplessness and control.

If one cannot make a difference to anyone, it is possible to become a tragic hero to oneself. If a person feels that he cannot effect a change in the other even if he gives fully and openly of himself sexually, he is involving himself in one of life's most frustrating experiences. On the other hand, one woman, because she could not accept the fact that she was a woman (like her mother) and really wanted to be a man (like her father), spent her sexual energies in arousing men, making them fall in love with her, but ultimately withholding from them. To make a difference to the other became her greatest triumph. To allow the other person to feel that he made a difference to her in the same way became her greatest defeat. Genuine reciprocity was truly impossible.

Laing again expresses this concept clearly:

> So-called hysterical frigidity in a woman is often based on refusal to allow any man the triumph of "giving" her satisfaction. Her frigidity is her triumph and her torment. The implication is, "You can have your penis, your erection, your orgasm, but it doesn't make any difference to me." And indeed, existentially speaking, ability to have an erection, to ejaculate with an orgasm, is only a very limited aspect of being potent. It is potency without power to make a difference to the other. A man who complains of impotence is

frequently a man who, analogously to the frigid hysterical woman, is determined not to give the woman the satisfaction of satisfying him.

Allowable sex refers to the sexual feelings which the person (self) feels safe in expressing to the real or imagined audience of his authority figures (others). Allowable sex is a concept that a child learns in the formative years. When the strategies of the parents are such that the child, in his counterstrategies, must go in an opposing direction, an internal conflict results that is usually accompanied by feelings of isolation. A simplistic example is that of a child who will not cross a street, even though it may appear quite safe to do so or even if his friends are crossing, because of his internalized feelings of prohibition on the part of the parental figures. A similar mechanism controls nonallowability of sexual expression except that, more often than not, the prohibition or disapproval by the parental figures in the sexual sphere is *implicit* rather than explicit. We pick up cues about what is, or is not, allowed from one parents' behavior as much as from their words. Their proscriptions about sex are often unexpressed to us because they could not even express them to themselves.

Allowable sex (that which the individual feels is "all he deserves to be allowed" to express sexually) may occur under certain specific conditions. It may be with another person or it may take the form of a masturbation fantasy. When there is conflict between what he cannot keep himself from expressing sexually and what he feels is allowable from the authority standard, the individual is possessed by strong guilt feelings. This can completely undermine his system of self-worth.

While allowable sex generally changes with age and experience, it is possible for an individual to become fixated at a certain point—for example, in the case of the voyeur. When a neurotic conflict resolution is made, the "treadmill" of the neuroses keeps the sexual problems at a generally fixed level. The patient's "allowable life" and his "allowable sex" are closely intertwined. The neurotic solutions allow the person to say, "This is the way I am. This is my fate."

Imagery provides a way to become aware of sexual conflicts, so a person can be liberated not only from false ideas about sex, but also from the false ways in which he has been defined that forced him eventually into the sexual difficulty. With awareness of these forces, he has the chance to opt for change.

I now suggest an imagery that may help you see your own limits of allowable sex.

You are to image a penis and a vagina.

Now you are to image an animal coming out of each.

Now have the two animals appear in a meadow and observe what they say and what they do.

The kinds of animals and what they do in the meadow will probably tell you something about your feelings about sex and sexuality. Can you connect this image to anything going on in your life right now? Does it have any meaning in terms of the past? Does it suggest some pattern of behavior? Some conflict?

Here are the responses of two people who helped me make a tape cassette on sexual imagery:

Cindy: An elephant coming out of the penis, and I didn't get anything coming out of the vagina. I got something–but I don't like it. [Laughs] I guess I have to say, even though I don't like it. It was an ant.

Shorr: Have the elephant and the ant appear in a meadow and tell me what they say and what they do.

Cindy: The elephant clomps into the meadow, and I mean big, as elephants do. And the little ant says [high squeaky voice], "No, no, please don't step on me, Mr. Elephant!" [Laughs]

Shorr: Does that have any meaning for you?

Cindy: Do you need to ask?

Shorr: It's a standard question.

Cindy: I think I'd have to further explain the images. They were very cartoony. The little ant came out of the vagina–just kind of stuck its feet over and looked out and about. The elephant was really weird because the penis was [laughs] a huge, long penis. And then it turned–the camera moved back and it turned into this big elephant. As to the meaning–these cartoon things pop up in my head a lot. I'm not taking it very seriously. I'm overpowered oftentimes as the image would reveal. I feel very small whenever I'm with a man and it's a sexual encounter.

Shorr: The all-powerful penis.

Cindy: Right. It really bugs me, and I'm trying to get out of that situation.

Shorr: Like it could overpower you or something?
Cindy: Or like I have no control of it.
Shorr: So the imagery is revealing some particular style of approach that you have in the sexual realm.
Cindy: Oh, absolutely!

Cindy was able to get in touch with a pattern of sexual behavior that she was not too happy about. This new awareness led to a new type of relationship with men.

Here, now, are Mike's responses to the same imagery:
Mike: I get a horse and a dove.
Shorr: The horse for . . . ?
Mike: The penis—the dove from the vagina.
Shorr: Have the horse and the dove appear in a meadow. What would they do, and how does it appear to you?
Mike: The horse just sort of clumps around, and the dove sits on the horse's rump—you know—like in a circus. They just sort of run around in the field. I guess the horse just lays down after a while.
Shorr: Does it have any meaning for you?
Mike: Yeah—I'm beginning to see my one-sidedness—the horse being the strong and the dove being the pretty, weak animal.
Shorr: Providing you with a role?
Mike: Exactly—which I hadn't realized.

Mike's responses to this imagery enabled him to recognize a pattern in his relationships with women. In an earlier part of the tape, he did the imagery of escorting female prisoners and other imageries which began to reveal his characteristic behavior. When he finished this one, he was able to make the connections between his first images and his later ones and to recognize some of the dynamics of his behavior.

The sexual imageries and questions should tell us:

1. How we define ourselves in relation to the opposite sex.
2. How we feel the opposite sex defines us.
3. The specific conflicts involved.
4. Our readiness to face the conflicts.
5. Finally, the degree to which we fear judgment on the part of others with regard to our sexual attitudes.

This is a good time for you to think back over your responses to the imageries in this chapter. If you have a written record, look it over. Do you have answers to any of the five questions? Do you begin to see a pattern in your own behavior? Are you nervous and afraid with the opposite sex? Are you confident? Do you feel you are constantly at a disadvantage? Or are you always trying to get the upper hand?

As you become aware of your sexual conflicts, you are in a position to begin to resolve them. And as you become more aware of your characteristic relationships with the opposite sex, you may find that you have been employing neurotic conflict resolutions and want to change them. Instead of having vague feelings of discomfort which you cannot identify, you are getting close to the heart of your problem and can take positive action to free yourself from destructive or defeating behavior.

Ask yourself: What is my most frequently repeated relationship with the opposite sex?

When I asked one woman this question, she said, "Forming the relationship and then dominating it; I had hoped my present relationship would be different. The more I control the relationships, the less happy they become."

A specific exercise to help expose your phenomenological world of sexual feeling is:

Imagine a sexual fantasy that a person of the opposite sex might have of you.

This can elicit a clear, idealized image of how you feel you must act in relation to the opposite sex and to the world. One man said, "She would want me to be a persuader of large crowds, of huge armies, and of large corporations." His response was evidence of his enormous need to control the world and nearly everyone in it.

A woman replied to the same imaginary situation, "I'm beautiful. He melts to my touch; his excitement and passion are aroused as he touches my sexual parts. No other woman in the world can excite him and give him such pleasure. He knows that no other woman in the world can love him with the depth of feeling I can offer."

Here are some statements that can expose your feelings about the opposite sex:

I have to prove to every woman (man) that ___.
The only good man (woman) is a ___.
Men (women), according to my mother, ___.
Never let a man (woman) ___.
I want a man (woman) to prove to me that ___.

The basic expectations which an individual relates to sex and intimacy undeniably have their roots in the family interactions of the past. One woman said in answer to the question, "Other women, according to my father, ______." ". . . were tramps, but I was a princess." Indeed, she tried to keep herself from men in a sexual way, and kept her purity and regality intact. This question obviously has many counterparts for both males and females. For example:

(Other) women, according to my mother,____.
(Other) men, according to my father,______.
(Other) men, according to my mother,______.

Typical responses that I have received to these questions are:

According to my mother, men (women)______________.

Responses

Female	*Male*
are beasts underneath; will never be true to you; can never be counted on.	are sacred objects; are not as good as she is; are less than men.

According to my father, men (women)______________.

Responses

Female	*Male*
were out to lay you; were not as nice as him; are only good to support you.	are strange; are no good; only want security.

Another imaginary situation which can be used to expose your inner world is the desert-island situation.

Imagine yourself on an island alone with a person of the opposite sex for an unknown time. How long will it be before sex will occur?

The answer invariably refers to how the other might think of you and your attractiveness. You will often include your fears and hesitancies and all of the strategies back and forth that might be involved.

Another excellent situation to yield inner conflicts that relate to a man's sexual feeling is:

Imagine you are a hummingbird and you are going to extract nectar from a flower. What would you do and what would you feel?

One thirty-five-year-old man answered, "I'd fly around and slowly put my beak into the flower and I'd find it closed. I fly around to many flowers and every time I'd try the flower would be closed. I'd get tired and fly away somewhere else."

I followed this response with a Finish the Statement, "If I am sexy, I'll ____________." He answered quickly and spontaneously, ". . . be punished."

When I ask a woman to imagine she is a flower and a hummingbird is alighting upon her, various answers that may directly relate to her sexual receptivity, or lack of it, are forthcoming. The responses range from ". . . love the feeling of the hummingbird's beak getting its nectar" to "...

somehow, the hummingbird just seems to hover over me and then goes on."

When I have asked the questions, "I go to men for ________," or "I go to women for ________," I have elicited sexual conflict areas, as well as how the person defines himself or feels he is being defined by others.

"I go to women *for approval*, but I go to men for *acknowledgment of my being a man*" was one man's response. Another man said, "I go to men for *approval* and I go to women for *revenge*."

I urge you to ask yourself these two questions. Completely honest answers will clarify your feelings about both sexes. They will certainly illustrate, more vividly than I can do here, the depth of feeling and awareness that imagery can reveal.

It may shock you to learn that your feelings of sexuality are not entirely your own. When I ask the question, "To whom do your sexual feelings belong?" the answer is nearly always ". . . to me, of course." But upon reflection, people become more aware of their feelings and the answer to this and related questions changes. For example, I may ask, "How much of your father still lives in you?" The reply may be "Seventy per cent me; thirty him." Or it may be "Only when I deal with women am I like him; otherwise not."

It is necessary to separate out your own sexual identity. You need to learn that you *can* make a difference to one of the opposite sex and still be your own person. Otherwise you will continue to be what you think the other wants and risk the loss of your own sexual identity. This can lead to a feeling of sexual responsibility to the other, perhaps to the point of being only a source of pleasure and neglecting your own gratification.

Some of the questions which can make you aware of your feelings in this area are:

What is your sexual responsibility to a woman (man)?

To whom does your penis (vagina) belong?

To whom do your love feelings belong?

To whom does your time belong?

To whom does your life belong?

It is sad to think of how many of us have fragmented ourselves and "sold" part of our feelings to another in order to survive.

Guilt plays an enormous role in sexual behavior. Remember, there is no guilt unless there is a standard for guilt. The behavior which is free and spontaneous in one family might be thought of as rigid and cause immobilization in another. Guilt is fundamental in the undermining process of the individual by the significant others in life. In time, the standard for guilt becomes absorbed and fixed, and any contrary behavior feels sneaky, anxiety-laden, and imbued with fear of exposure. The standard for guilt which we acquire seems final beyond questioning, and doubt of the standard only leads to greater guilt, which leads to further compliance and "good" behavior. Finally, if the process does not allow a glimmer of protest, detachment results. According to Victor Frankl in *Man's Search for Meaning*, we all need to learn that it is "... a perogative of man to become guilty—and his responsibility to overcome guilt."

The conflict between the natural expression of sexual feelings and the devious ways in which the individual was forced to express sexuality often are symbolized in the "first lie about sex" reaction.

Ask yourself: "What was your first lie about sex?"

Often I hear of incidents from childhood. A common one involves playing the game of "doctor" or "discovery" with an adventurous playmate of the opposite sex. When a child is found at this kind of play, he fabricates a lie to cover up something he senses is "wrong," even though he doesn't know why. Such incidents of childhood, involving the feeling of wrongdoing to an absolute authority standard, are capable of evoking pain or guilt feelings years later in the adult.

Perhaps you won't remember your first lie about sex, but will recall some other significant event. For example, one man replied, "I don't remember my first lie about sex, but I do remember the time I lied about being found in this girl's room at college, and the dean wrote to my parents. Boy, I had to talk my way out of that one!"

You need to find out how guilt has been induced into you and the effect it has had in undermining you. It can be present to such an overwhelming degree that it may cripple your functioning and fragment your relations to the world. To help you probe the roots of your guilt and to find ways to free yourself, answer the following questions:

What do you feel most guilty about?

To whose standard of guilt do you respond?

Closely allied with guilt is, of course, the accounting to the authority person. When a person, while engaged in sex, acts as though he is robbing a safe, we can be sure that his "lookout" for the police and his "getaway car" are not far away. One of the best questions for eliciting this reaction is:

In whose presence do you feel the greatest turn-off of your sexuality?

"In front of my mother," a twenty-year-old answered. "And it's the same with Mary." (He and Mary were living together.) "Like, I get angry at Mary when I've been at a bar with the boys and she questions me because I'm a little late. It's like she's omniscient—she's everywhere, she can see all and knows I've done bad, regardless."

Another method of revealing awareness of our accountability to some authority figure is the question:

Imagine yourself in a "morality" witness box and accuse the accusers.

This may help you learn to account to your own concept of morality and not to a concept of morality alien to your genuine feelings. The alien morality has been imposed upon you by others. When you can recognize this, you can free yourself of it.

This chapter does not pretend to discuss exhaustively the internal conflicts related to sexuality. Its purpose is merely to demonstrate the method of applying Psycho-Imagination techniques in the context of some specific sexual conflicts that I have found among my patients. The aim of Psycho-Imagination Therapy is to help you become aware of the discrepancy between your definition of yourself and the false definition your significant others hold of you. When this awareness is acute and when the sense of your true identity becomes stronger, you can attempt to change the other person's definition of you.

CHAPTER VII

Transforming and Focusing for Change

How often have you said to yourself, "If only I could relive that experience, I would do it differently this time!"?

In a sense, that is the operational definition of Task Imagery. An imaginary situation which involves you in a task, or a job, or a way of doing something is a Task Image. Your response to the task can reveal characteristic styles of action and reaction. You can become aware of patterns in your behavior—how you go about performing jobs; how you relate to authority; your attitudes about various activities.

If your initial response to one of the following image examples indicates a generally acceptable self-concept and good interpersonal self-definition, there is no need to do the imagery sequence a second time. It felt "good," so there is no need to transform the image. If, however, the first response indicates a way of being that you are not satisfied with, then the image can be redone. By experiencing a Task Imagery a second, or even a third time, you can find new modes of behavior—better ways of accomplishing the task—and carry the new actions and attitudes into the real world of experience. Task Imagery has a reparative quality, and it helps you feel better as your conflicts are resolved.

I have seen people learn through Task Imagery how to bolster their courage to fight life's battles; how to increase their control over themselves, as well as over outside forces; and how to develop the strength to fight guilt and shame and to create order out of disorder. Task Imagery helps them draw on the power and energy that exist within every human being.

While it is true that all of these things are possible, remember that you must be *ready* to change. There are several elements that are needed to reach that state of readiness: you must be aware of your internal conflicts; you need to be in touch with the feelings and emotions that come from traumatic incidents; you must recognize undermining strategies used by the significant people in your life; and you must recognize your own counterstrategies or defenses.

As an example, I suggest you try the following Task Imagery. Let your imagery flow, and trust your experiences and feelings.

Imagine climbing one thousand steps to the top.

As you undertake this imaginary task, you probably are revealing a particular style or attitude of approach. You may express doubts, or you may have a feeling of mastery.

As you proceed up the stairs, do you meet other people? Do you make it all the way to the top? What happened on the way? What happened at the top?

Some people cannot go up more than 90 per cent; others take the steps two at a time to reach the top rapidly. One woman reached the top readily enough, then held her hands high above her head and spoke of meeting the Archangel Gabriel and a host of other angels, all of whom clamored for her to perform as if on a stage.

Were you surprised by what happened as you ascended? Many people are. Sometimes repressed feelings emerge. These feelings may indicate the degree of hopelessness or optimism in your life.

There may have been some point in your ascent where you did not like yourself. You were faced with a negative self-concept. This is the time to confront the despised self-image and transform it. If your negative image was revealed through interaction with persons you encountered who blocked your way, this is an appropriate moment to have yourself confront the others through imagery in a way that will allow you to view yourself in a more favorable light.

Suppose, for example, you imagine a person in your climb who tries to prevent your progress, or who makes negative remarks to you. In re-experiencing the imagery, face the person who is defining you incorrectly and finish the sentences:

I am not ______________________________!
I am __________________________________!

In so doing, raise your voice. You must feel what you say. Repeat your statement, and, if need be, scream! Do not allow yourself to be incorrectly defined by others. It is also important to you to know who those others are and what they mean to you.

Instead of persons who are negative forces in your life, the thousand-steps imagery may reveal those who are positive forces in relation to you—people who care about you, who see you as you really are.

Look for indications of achievement and assertion in the imagery. Do you have an overzealous or overwhelming desire for achievement? Do you assert yourself at the appropriate time?

If you weren't happy with your original response to the thousand-steps exercise, see if you can do it again in a more satisfying way.

If there is no appreciable change in the image at this moment, do it again in a few days. This may be more fruitful, or you may have to wait even longer. You do have to get to the point of readiness. Your motivation to change a painful state is vital.

Remember, the very process of repeating the imagery flow in a healthier direction can help you to change your attitude and behavior in life situations. Changed imagery experience often leads to changed behavior.

As you can see with just this one example, Task Imagery can show your characteristic styles of behavior, how you view yourself and others, and it can provide clues to possible conflicts within yourself.

In essence, any imaginary situation contains the possibility of revealing conflicts and the individual's style of behavior. Each situation provides insight into self-definition *and* can also be a vehicle for changing the self-image. After all, they are your images; they come from within you. Therefore, they are yours to transform. If I were to ask you to imagine yourself as an animal and your image were an ant or a mouse, you might be feeling weak, powerless, dissatisfied. But you could work at changing that image. You could transform yourself into an elephant, or a tiger, or the biggest mouse in the world. As you do and redo the image and come to accept it, you will begin to notice changes in your actions and attitudes.

Certain Task Imageries may have more impact than others. Each of us reacts differently, according to our situation at that time and also past experience.

Perhaps you will learn more about yourself in the following Task Imagery.

Imagine building a bridge across a gorge.

What kind of a bridge did you build? Did you do it alone or with help? Did you complete the task? How deep was the gorge? How long was your bridge? Can you cross the completed bridge?

A thirty-year-old woman responding to this imagery learned something about herself. Here is a verbatim report:

Cassandra: I got a very simple bridge. Wooden stakes that I'd driven into the ground clear across the gorge and a burlap material with ropes as handholds.

Shorr: How big is the bridge and how deep is the gorge?

Cassandra: It's long and it's high—one hundred feet long and thirty to forty feet high. Enough to make you queasy. I could walk across easily. I have a fear of heights, and by the time I got over I would have conquered the height fear.

Shorr: The style and characteristic of it—does that indicate anything about you?

Cassandra: Well—it was rather primitive and basic. Seems very high to me. That indicates to me that my goals and desires are high—not easily attainable, but worthy goals. And I am rather basic. I'm basic and earthy, and the bridge is made of wood, mud, clay, burlap, and rope—all things that are basically down-to-earth.

Shorr: Can you redo the bridge in imagery?

Cassandra: Yes. Now I'm thoroughly comfortable, but if I were to change it, it would be a low arc—a Japanese bridge—a wooden one you just walk across—down on the ground. Delicate and spiritual.

Shorr: Which do you like better?

Cassandra: I like them both. The first is more interesting and exciting because of the height. But I like the lazy, peaceful strolling across the delicate, intricately carved bridge.

Shorr: Which is more consistent with your true identity?

Cassandra: I guess I would have to say the first one is the basic me, and the second is myself developed to a higher level.

Shorr: Which do you want the world to see?

Cassandra: The first one. Redoing made me discover that there is that possibility I don't want to hide that little core. I thought I wanted to hide it.

Here is another response to the same image exercise. Bill is a thirty-year-old man.

Bill: First I would be in great despair. The gorge would be a little too deep and too wide for me to build a bridge. But I would have to build it because there is something on the other side that I want. It would take three or four days to get around to it. While I'm building it, I'm making sure it can be used many, many more times. I don't want to build a dumb bridge. There's no point in doing it, and whatever is on the other side will be there when I get there. I make sure it will be solid. Lots of lumber and tree trunks. And the more I get into it the faster I build it until it's completed in less time than I thought it would take. But I would make very sure that it would be sturdy and that it would satisfy me very much and other people could say, "Hey, you really built a terrific bridge." That would be important to me also.

Shorr: Can you redo the bridge?

Bill: I can, but I don't know that it would be necessary.

Shorr: What does it indicate about your characteristic style?

Bill: It's so clear to me. First I don't like to do anything until I have to—until there's such a damn good reason for doing it. Then I have to force myself into it, and somehow or other I get it done. The problem is not the bridge, but how much enjoyment I get out of it. I could get more pleasure building Cassandra's bridge for her. I'd get a great deal of pleasure doing it for her.

There is no limit to the number of Task Imageries that can be used in the same way as the thousand-steps and the bridge images are used. Each may have its own impact upon you, depending upon your particular circumstances and experience.

Here is a Task Image which deals with another aspect of your personality:

Imagine that you start riding a child-size train and then imagine it transformed into a large locomotive.

How did you feel when you were riding the small train? Did you feel small also? What happened when you transformed the train into a large locomotive? Did you begin to feel some power in riding on the large train? Did you feel strength and power while changing the small train to a big one?

Try to remember your feelings as you did that

image and then compare those feelings with what you experience as you do the next Task Image.

Imagine an animal in your guts. If it is a rabbit, a snake, or some other weak or negative animal, concentrate on transforming it into a more positive or a stronger image.

In both of these images you are attempting to transform weak or negative images into strong or positive ones. It may not be easy the first time you attempt the change, but as you continue to struggle you will find hidden strengths. Never forget that these are your images, and no one can prevent you from changing them. You created them and you can erase them; change all or part of them; use anything to help you.

The metamorphosis that takes place in your imagery can be carried over into the world of experience.

Perhaps you are looking for a way to gain greater control of your world and of overpowering forces within it. Try this Task Image:

Imagine you are driving a Sherman tank across a bumpy field.

How did you feel maneuvering that big tank? Did it give you a feeling of control? You were in a position to decide whether to smash through obstacles or go around them. You were in a vehicle which had the potential to destroy or overcome whatever was in front of it. Can you put some of that feeling to work for you in overcoming the obstacles in your life?

Now try this image:

Imagine you have a housewrecker's large steel ball and can make it break brick buildings, etc.

How did you feel? Did you like what you were doing? Did either of these two images help you to release some of the anger you were feeling? Go with your feelings and see if you can't capture the sense of being in control and use that sense when you want to.

Now I would like you to try a different type of Task Image. See what you can learn from it.

Imagine cleaning an oily, scaly piece of metal.

How did you go about the task? Were you able to accomplish it? Did it give you a sense of satisfaction? Was the way you tackled the job characteristic of how you usually do things of that nature?

That image refers to the way you go about bringing order out of disorder. If you usually fly to pieces or become frustrated, then that is probably what happened in your imagery. If that happened, I suggest you do the image again, and this time try a more studied, reasonable approach. When you have accomplished this task, go on to the next one:

Imagine unraveling a knotty rope.

Are you finding it easier to create order out of chaos? Keep trying–the reward is well worth the effort.

Very often, people have the feeling that they are losing the fight against powerful forces. I usually have them try the next Task Image:

Imagine you are herding a bunch of horses into a corral one mile away.

What happened? Were you able to do what you attempted? How long did it take? Were there obstacles to overcome? How was your response to this image similar to your characteristic way of doing a difficult task?

Here is a report of one man's struggle with that image:

> I'm in the country with rolling hills all around. I can see my destination ahead, and it really looks far away. I'm a little unsure how to begin, so I mount one of the horses thinking that the rest would follow. It's not working at all. I'll try to herd them from behind. I'm riding around the back perimeter of the group, hoping to push them as a group forward. This doesn't even begin to work. I'm getting frustrated. I feel like someone has trusted me to complete this job, and I can't even get started. It's an easy job it seems, but I can't do it. I again ride around the back of them all, trying to move them forward, but nothing. They won't budge. I can see them eating and not even noticing my presence. I'm really frustrated now. It's now like a mental block. There is no fuckin' way those horses are going to move for me.
>
> What started out to be a seemingly simple request is now totally impossible. I can't even force my mind to see them walking or running for-

> ward. They just won't move. I feel terrible. Joe asked me to imagine this and I can't even begin to do it. I can't do it, Joe, they won't move.

At this point I told him to take charge of the situation.

> The very second you said "Take charge," I ran up to the horses with confidence to move mountains, and started to slap them on the ass saying, "Come on, you sons-of-bitches, get going." I'm running around slapping them on the butt and they are all going. I'm really in charge of the total situation. I can feel the confidence with every slap. "Come on, you sons-of-bitches, let's get going."
>
> I can see the group of horses all paying close attention to what I want them to do. I've got them all running together towards the pen a mile away. I remount my horse and ride alongside of them, occasionally slapping one that gets out of the main group.
>
> Now I can see them all running into the pen and I close the gate behind them feeling good. I put my horse in a separate stable and give him a pat of appreciation as I walk away.

This is a clear example of what the image may reveal. It also demonstrates how to transform images so they are more consistent with our attempts to change. When the man first imagined the task, he was powerless, frustrated, blocked. He was so caught by those feelings, he did not even look for another way to accomplish his task. Only when I urged him to take charge of the situation did he begin to use his inner resources.

When you first do an image—Task, Body, Self,

or Dual—you are told to just let it flow and see what meaning you can get from it. Whether it reveals a new truth, or merely confirms one you have recognized and tried to avoid, once you have realized what it is telling you about yourself, you are in a position to work with it, change it, recreate it.

Here is still another kind of Task Imagery. Try it, search out its meaning, then transform it if need be.

Imagine you are leading some people out of a swamp.

Were you successful? Did the others accept your leadership? Did you feel good about leading or were you hesitant, unsure of yourself? This image shows how well you can rescue yourself and others from danger. It demonstrates what you do and feel when you are in a position to be a leader.

It may be true that you are fine when you have to rescue others, but you are not so confident when you are trying to overcome danger to yourself. Here is a test of how you fight for yourself:

Imagine you are removing the fuse from a live bomb.

Were you more successful or less, with this task than you were with the swamp? Can you see a difference in your motivation? Are you better when you have to perform for others, or do you have doubts and fears when you feel you are being judged?

Task Imagery involves the formation of reconstructions. You can also add enlightening new insights through a rearrangement of connections in the process of redoing the imagery. You gain positive contribution to self-esteem as you complete the task successfully. Invariably this is also an emotional experience. The task plus the emotion involved helps you change your self-image.

Throughout this book as you have done various images, I have asked, "How did you feel?" The feelings that are evoked by your imagery are vital to the whole process. Re-experiencing the old feelings that led to the development of strategies and defenses you want to be rid of is the first step toward change.

We come now to a Task Imagery that one does not enter lightly. I do not recommend that you engage in this image unless you feel ready for it. It relates to those of you who feel so rotten that you are constantly afraid that your rotten self will be exposed to others. Those who are overwhelmed with guilt can sometimes relieve that feeling by doing the following:

Imagine that you are in a sewer full of rats and you are walking through this foul-smelling atmosphere. Do not yield to the foul atmosphere and the rats, but fight your way out to a safe place and then clean yourself.

If you do not allow yourself to be engulfed by the sewer and the rats, you are allowing yourself to fight your rottenness and to eliminate it. I encourage you not to give in to your rotten feelings. Transform them!

In doing Task Imagery, you are overcoming

one or more conflicts, changing a poor self-definition, or refuting an alien identity. The courage you exhibit in doing the task enhances your self-image as you see the truth about yourself. Task Imagery generally involves anxiety and risk taking. The more thoroughly you master the Task Imagery, the more solid is the resolution of the conflict. It is an act of creation. New outcomes and new points of view emerge as you relive and redo Task Imagery.

Now try this image:

Imagine you are a fetus about to birth.

How do you feel? Did you experience some powerful emotions?

Some people seem not to want to give birth to themselves; others relate directly to their own birth from their mother's uterus and express some of their strongest feelings, imagining their parents' respective attitudes to the event. The awareness that they were unwanted may emerge. Still others react with hostility as they imagine the task. One man desired to "... crawl on all fours away from my parents so that they can never find me."

A common reaction is the sense of being born anew, with new possibilities in life. But the spectrum of response is limitless; rarely does this task fail to evoke strong feelings. As with other forms of imagery, this one can lead to a sequence of images or reminiscences that are a basis for change.

Some persons don't want to leave the warmth of the womb. One man expressed it this way:

I find myself in a womb. It is comfortable, warm, and secure. I begin to feel an ever-mounting pressure pushing me down towards the vagina. I resist. I prop my hands and feet against the lower wall so as not to be pushed out. Great fear overwhelms me as I realize that I don't have the strength to resist.

As my head exits, the fear diminishes quite a bit. All of a sudden, I plop out. Fear has left me and I feel angry at those handling me so roughly, but I no longer feel afraid. In fact, I am amused at my previous fears.

I feel that I am always afraid of transitions. I fear the event most before it happens rather than when it actually does come about. I frequently feel joy after having survived through such emotions.

Sometimes in therapy I may "force" the person to make the attempt to birth, supportively urging him on. For some people, this represents the choice they must make in order to establish a new self-concept. Facing their feelings of "rottenness" and now allowing themselves to deserve are important elements of this Task Imagery.

Others recreate their own actual birth scene, experiencing pain or pleasure and recounting imaginary dialogues with their mothers and fathers. Feelings abandoned early in life may return with force, clarifying some heretofore hidden self-concept.

You have already done two Task Images that relate to gaining control of your world. Here is one that I use frequently with people who fear losing control or must have control at all costs.

Imagine backing through a paper wall.

What happened? What kind of paper wall did you visualize? Was the task easy or difficult? One of my patients wrote the following account of his image of backing through a paper wall:

> When Joe asked me to try walking backwards through a wall, it came to be an effort filled with uncertainty and a sort of coercion. I didn't find it impossible to image—just something I didn't want to do. In typical fashion I felt somewhat compelled to co-operate with Joe and then imagine.
>
> I described the wall as rice-paper thin and brittle, so that my backing through it left a "trace outline" of my body as I *fell*. I tried to image several times. First I fell endlessly into space. Next, I "hinged" over like a domino and slammed onto cold concrete. When Joe suggested the possibility of some action or result less harsh, I plopped onto a huge iced cake.
>
> Regardless of the number of times I tried (or now try) the image, walking backwards was very uncomfortable. The result of falling may carry different degrees of impact, all somewhat uncomfortable, but the *process of falling* is always terrifying.
>
> I'm going to just throw out feelings and thoughts on the image as they come to me. My discomfort in falling, the falling itself, indicates much need to foresee my circumstances. The wall is the future, the unforeseeable. The wall is frail because the unforeseen is very threatening to me. My body outline left in the wall seems to me to indicate how real that fear is. It's not some vague impression, but a sharp picture of the whole "me." I have a large stake in the need to see

the future, to be in control, and the control is a delicate thing (like the rice paper). Although I can imagine that other people might see floating through the wall and up into some person's arms for example. I *fall. Falling is failing.* Because I don't know what it is I'm getting into, I can't stand up or be in balance. And not being on balance or in control is failing. (For that matter, loss of control and failing occur in the image of walking *forward*—though with a different twist.) If the wall were not in the image, but I just walked backwards, I would still fall, assuming that the walking backwards means not looking over the shoulder.

I can imagine another person's image being quite different as in the example above, but fear of failure and lack of belief in myself is too strong. To succeed under the conditions of the image, or even to fail understandably and without regret, is incomprehensible to me at this time.

As for walking forward, it is more comfortable, but not much. The comfort is really an illusion based on the idea of some foreseeability and/or a sort of masochistic abandon. I feel, as I aggressively break through the wall headfirst, that somehow, in falling, I can see wherever the hell I'm going, even though I'm out of control. The wall is more like cardboard in this image. It represents a substance more thick and malleable, reflecting that minor degree of control in being somewhat prepared for the fall. But once through that wall, the result is substantially the same. As I imaged with Joe before, I go defiantly headfirst through the wall, but then I image being in that falling space or smacking into a brick wall. As I mentioned above, the forward walk is off balance, out of control (stumbling), and so again indicates the fear of failure due to unpreparedness.

I'm getting tired of this fear of failing.

An interesting contrast came from trying to image going *to* this place *on the other side.* It really doesn't matter whether what awaits me on the other side is a beautiful beach (as we tried) or a grotesque monster. That image situation is very different and more comfortable *because* I know what awaits me. I can try to prepare myself and thus the fear of failing, that anxiety, is within my control.

My other-oriented existence is so strong, my "self" so incapable, that the wall of uncertainty leaves little or no chance for taking delight in the unexpected because it may cause me to fail and thus embarrass myself in "others' " eyes.

I used to think I was so ready for adventure, ready to try anything. But I couldn't quite understand why it was that I would feel uneasy in a situation of isolation such as camping *alone*, or traveling abroad *with* someone but in a *foreign* situation–basically taking a chance. I think I'm talking about dependency here, on Dad, on others, but not on myself, because I am not worthwhile, good enough to depend on myself in unfamiliar circumstances.

Maybe backing through the image often enough will lead to more ease in the unknown, the risky, will cause me to emerge either victorious, or unembarrassed and confident in defeat.

If you are suffering from a feeling of powerlessness, you can try this image to fight that feeling:

Imagine you have the strongest hands in the world. Make sure you have the feeling. Now imagine squeezing or tearing various things, starting with a telephone book and progressing to the neck of a lion.

I urge you to throw yourself into this image. Really experience what you are visualizing. Then try to capture that feeling of power and divert it to use in your life.

If you feel better as a result of these experiences, I suggest you try to connect your strengthened feeling to specific *human* situations in which you have been defined by others.

Emotionally connecting your strength in relation to *human* experiences and the way you have been defined is of the utmost importance. Otherwise, the strengthening that may occur is not directed for change, and the techniques suggested here become interesting, but useless, exercises.

William James, the great psychologist who lived at the turn of the century, said in *Principles in Psychology*:

> If we wish to conquer undesirable emotional tendencies in ourselves we must assiduously, and in the first instance cold-bloodedly, go through the outward movements of these contrary dispositions which we prefer to cultivate.

He is suggesting rehearsing the emotions and feelings so that they become familiar to us. Imagery can help us in the same fashion. Through Imagery we can redo tasks until they are satisfying—until they reflect the kind of image we want of ourselves. We rehearse the desired behavior in imagery just as we rehearse desired dispositions. The rehearsals help us to transform our actions and our self-image. Gardner Murphy in *Personality*, in 1947, anticipated the concept of transformation of imagery when he stated, "But images . . . are manipulable just as are muscular acts, to give new and better satisfactions."

By repeating an imaginary situation, you can increase the intensity of the desired response, focusing for greater feeling each time. This is especially true when the image seems devoid of emotion. As an example, I once asked a man "to imagine two different rocking chairs and then to imagine somebody different in each." He imagined an old man in one rocking chair and a young man in the other. I then instructed him to make a statement to each of the men. He started with an abstract statement in his initial response. His second response was a factual statement about the furniture. I repeated the imaginary situation, urging him to make an emotional statement to each man. This time he showed more emotion in his statements and expressed some concern about "the older man's son who was lost in Vietnam." From this initial spark, more profound expressions of feelings emerged.

Some people present an image world which is essentially flat and impoverished. Such patients tend to complain that they feel empty, unsubstantial, unreal, a meaningless bundle of discontinuous bits and pieces. When their image world comes to life, when they relate to the emotional content, they often have, for the first time, a pleasant sense of possessing a separate and unique identity. They feel that they are, in truth, less vulnerable and helpless than they used to consider themselves.

I cannot stress too strongly the importance of

emotions. The prime value of imagery lies in stimulating associations and evoking emotions. The imaginary situations are neither parlor games nor intellectual exercises. They are designed to conjure up the feelings which lead to awareness of old patterns of behavior and to new insights. Once you are in touch with your true feelings, you are in a position to transform them if they are inadequate, inappropriate, or unsatisfying.

Powerful emotion is often released when you use your imagination in creative visualizations. The content of these waking imageries is often symbolic of situations in your life—past or present—and as you experience them, you will activate repressed feelings associated with those situations. Many therapists have recognized the importance of triggering these associations through imagery. Erich Fromm wrote:

> There are other active methods to stimulate free association. Let us assume you have analyzed the patient's relationship to his father, but want more unconscious material than he has offered in his associations; you tell the patient: "Now concentrate on the picture of your father, and tell me what is the first thing that comes to your mind." I might draw your attention to the fact that there is a certain difference between asking the patient, "What comes to your mind about your father?" and the second way of telling him: "Now concentrate, focus on your father." Or "Visualize your father now, and tell me what is on your mind." There seems to be only a slight difference in wording. However, there is a very great difference in the effect.
>
> Another way of stimulating free association lies

> in giving the patient the picture of a certain situation, then asking what comes to his mind. For instance, you can tell the patient: "Assume tomorrow morning your telephone rings and the person calling tells you I have died. What comes to mind?" Well, you will find that there are very interesting free associations which come up.

Rehearsing behavior and emotions in imagery can be a powerful aid in changing your life. As you transform your images, you learn how to transform your actions. As you rehearse appropriate emotions, you learn where and when they are appropriate. When you imagine the worst possible outcome of a dilemma, you may find you are better able to cope than you had previously thought. Rehearsal in imagination provides encouragement for later implementation of real behavior.

There is evidence that rehearsal of behavior can be used in numerous ways. In addition to overcoming destructive actions, it is beneficial at times in reinforcing a particular skill. For example, Dr. Richard Suinn of Colorado State University uses it to help athletes prepare for competition. He has them first relax and then imagine competing in the actual event. Skiers see themselves at the top of the slalom course just before the start of a race and then run the course through imagery. The experience is so real that the skier responds with many of the sensations he would have in actual competition. He hears the crunch of snow under his skis, he feels the wind on his face, his muscles twitch as if they are being used. His feet often turn in the direction he imagines he is skiing. Various ski championships won by his students have proved the value of this type of training.

The same process works for other sports as well. Wrestlers, ballplayers, and swimmers have found it effective. Perhaps you can use it to improve your golf or tennis game.

Rehearsal behavior need not be confined to improving sports skills. It may prove helpful for any activity that requires constant practice. A famous ballerina was once hospitalized for many months following an automobile accident. She lay immobilized in traction, able to move only her fingers. She rehearsed her dance roles in her imagination, doing the steps with her fingers. When she was able to return to the stage, she said it was fairly simple to pick up where she had left off. In fact, she felt that many of her routines were improved.

There are other ways of bringing about desired changes in behavior, attitudes, and feelings. The Most and Least Question can be utilized as a way of focusing and sharpening psychological events in your life. For example, ask yourself:

What is the most exciting year of your life? Take your time and see if you can reminisce and concretize that particular time.

My guess is that for most of you this is not too difficult. Moving to a more difficult Most and Least Question, ask yourself:

What was the single most traumatic event of your childhood?

Does this question bring up lots of strong feelings? Even if it happened long ago, does it still affect you?

My experience indicates that some significant person in your life was probably involved with you. If such a person treated you unfairly, cruelly, or violently, I would like to introduce you to Cathartic Imagery.

First a word of caution. Cathartic Imagery is not easy since it demands you to mobilize emotions heretofore either buried, or which, if expressed—as in the case of anger—made you feel guilty. Cathartic Imagery demands that the other person regard you in a different light from that which he or she has ascribed to you.

As a child, if you got angry at your parents, however justified you were, they usually made you feel guilty. Cathartic Imagery means imagining parents, or other significant persons, in front of you and requires you to liberate yourself from their definition of you—but without guilt.

Return to the traumatic incident for a moment. Reimagine it in your mind and then to that other person say loudly, "Don't you ever refer to me as ____________!" Finish the sentence simply and clearly.

One of my patients was able to confront an imagined parent with such a statement. "Don't you ever call me ungrateful," he screamed at the imaged father who had used such an accusation against him.

The goal is liberating oneself from a false accusation. The majority of people who are intensely angry with someone are able to work through their anger by fantasizing an active expression of it toward the target person. But there are some who must express it in a person-to-person confrontation. Even if the imagined confrontation is insufficient to resolve the anger, the fantasizing can be a useful bridge into actual confrontation.

At times, everyone has an overwhelming desire to scream, "I am not who you say I am! I am somebody completely different!" No doubt you have felt that way many times in your life, but it was not feasible, or you lacked the courage, to scream.

In Psycho-Imagination Therapy, the major emphasis is on *not* allowing others to define us differently from our real selves. Focusing on asserting one's real self sometimes takes a little screaming. I do not believe in screaming just for the sake of screaming. However, screaming in the service of an indignant ego that will no longer be misinterpreted or misdefined is central to focusing for change.

Essentially there are two approaches to the statements that emerge as screams. The first are those statements said to the other about the other. This requires us to imagine the face and body of someone who has defined us incorrectly.

Close your eyes and imagine that person. Try to remember some negative accusation that was made against you that was not true. Try especially to relate it to some *non sequitur* character assassination like "selfish," "lazy," "uncaring," etc., which is hard to disprove though untrue. Now, to that person, scream:

Don't you dare ____________________!
Don't you ever ____________________!
Never refer to me as ________________!

How did that feel? Are you satisfied? If not, do it again, only louder, sustaining your autonomy as a person. Look the one who misdefines you in the eyes. DO NOT BEG!

Let us go to the second set of sentences that are said to the other about oneself:

Focusing on the target person, make these statements count in asserting your real self:

I am not ______________________________!
I am ________________________________!
The best thing about me is ______________!
I am convinced that I __________________!

There is no formula for bringing about change. But there are certain necessary steps and ingredients. First you must be motivated—must want to change. And you must be ready for change. You must focus on what you want to change. Let your imagery flow to help you become aware of your conflicts, your defenses, your alien identity, your feelings of rottenness. Then redo the images in a way consistent with the new person you want to be. Constantly check your feelings and if they are negative, unsatisfactory, work at changing them through your imagery. Rehearse in imagery what you hope to be in the world of actual experience.

When you have learned to apply these approaches, you will be able to mobilize the constructive and creative forces within you. All of this will be energized on your own behalf.

Liberating ourselves from an alien identity allows us to be what we are all striving to be—more human, and namely, ourselves.

CHAPTER VIII

Castles in the Air, Marble Halls, and Sealed Cans under Water

At one point during Walter Shirra's Mercury Space Flight, NASA observers in Houston were unable to make contact with him. Repeated signals went unanswered and there was concern that something had happened either to the astronaut, the spacecraft, or the telemetry. Everyone experienced great relief when it was learned that Shirra was unaware that he had been called because he had been lost in a daydream.

Whether you call them reveries, fantasies, castles in the air, or daydreams, no doubt you too have been so rapt by an internal vision that you have failed to respond to external stimuli. You may have neglected to answer your spouse because you were wool-gathering; failed to hear the doorbell because you were developing a happier outcome to your recent interchange with your boss;

or suddenly discovered that you had arrived at your destination with no recollection of how you drove there because your mind was wandering.

Daydreams may be wish-fulfillment fantasies, ego-enhancing reveries, or even negative imaginings of events that are sources of fear or anxiety. They seem to occur most often during times when the external environment is tedious or frustrating. They are a turning away from the outer world to inner visions—to a private world of grandiose achievements and captivating experiences.

Frustrations, both the minor ones of the day and the major ones of life, are common themes in daydreams. Very often the daydreams help us to bear existing tensions and frustrations while simultaneously exploring ways of relieving them.

Daydreams may take the form of rehearsal of anticipated events, interior monologues or dialogues, or fantastic dramas. You may be unaware how much daydreaming you actually do. Clinical experiments have shown a link between creativity, curiosity, imagination, artistic or scientific ability, and daydreaming. The connection is difficult to define exactly—perhaps the chronic daydreamer is more willing to flow with originality and creativity.

In the early 1920s, J. Varendonck undertook a systematic study of his daydreams. Whenever he caught himself wool-gathering he would trace back the chain of thought that had started the reverie. He discovered that the daydreams generally touched on matters of personal importance and, further, that they originated both from external stimuli and spontaneous memories. His daydreams often revolved around worries, or interests, or pleasant wishes that he could imagine fulfilled.

Very little further study of daydreaming was done until Jerome L. Singer, a Yale psychology professor, began examining his own daydreams for meaning. In 1966 he published a book on his findings. (It had taken nearly half a century for daydreams to be considered a fit subject for study.)

Although daydreams, imagination, and imagery are often treated as though they are all the same process, I prefer to make a distinction between daydreams and waking imagery. The daydream often has a story quality, it begins and ends; and it usually has a definitive theme. Not so, always, with waking imagery. There we have a constant flow of pictures, thoughts, feelings, etc., fleeting, fragmentary, and kaleidoscopic. They can be directed, however, so that they become clear pictures with meaning, very much like daydreams.

I do not ignore daydreams in my work. On the contrary, when patients reveal their daydreams to me, I treat them with respect and work with them just as I do with dreams and with waking images.

You, of course, can do the same. Search your daydreams for recurring themes, for indications of unresolved conflicts, for unfulfilled wishes, and for the strategies you use to deal with the fantasized events.

As important as daydreams are for revealing tensions, frustrations, and repressed material, those dreams you have while sleeping are even more valuable. Your thoughts and images unfold in your dreams with less censorship than your waking thoughts. There is less self-deception and less need to maintain the image you present to the world. No matter how bizarre the dreams, you can disavow responsibility and say, "It was just a dream."

It is inconceivable to imagine a dream that is not composed of images: visual, auditory, tactile, or gustatory. Dreams are without doubt some of the most important indicators of your phenomenological world. They are full of all sorts of images, and our job is to find meaning in them even though they may appear strange and unrelated. Your dreams originate out of your private world of experience just as your waking images do. Therefore, both are capable of revealing information about you that bypasses your censorship.

Before you actually start working with your dreams, you will want to keep a few important things in mind. Essentially, you are looking for your self-definition, how you are defined by others, the strategies you use to maintain your identity, repressed material, characteristic patterns of behavior, and areas of conflict.

The happenings in your daily life and the fleeting thoughts and images that flash through your mind often furnish the material for your dreams. Tensions, frustrations, problems may surface to be dealt with in dreams. The same feelings and emotions that occur in waking life also occur in dreams, but often the dreams help us to pinpoint their sources.

Have you ever awakened with the recollection of a dream fragment? Just a fleeting image of someone or something? I'm sure you have—many times. We dream intermittently throughout the night and remember only a portion of our dreams. Possibly the reason we remember certain dream fragments is because we may be blocking on the total dream. These fragments can be examined and interpreted. There are numerous ways to get meaning from dream fragments. Freud dealt with dream fragments by asking his patients to free associate to the remembered fragment and then to give him a verbal report of the associations. He found this approach fruitful.

I think even more pertinent material is elicited when you take the remembered fragment and associate images to it. This usually leads to more uncovering and more feeling than verbal reports do.

In essence, I suggest that you allow spontaneous images to flow from the original fragment. Just let yourself go. The entire sequence will usually have a pattern of meaning for you. You may be amazed at the rich and unsuspected insights yielded in this type of image association.

Looking back historically, we find that soon after Freud abandoned his concentration technique of eliciting patients' imagery, he published his monumental work, *The Interpretation of Dreams*. Rather than negating imagery, psychoanalysis retained its interest in imagery primarily through dreams.

C. G. Jung suggested that in the therapy session, the dream be continued beyond its actual termination; that the patient be encouraged to imagine the consequences that might occur from this further development of the "story."

Both Freud and Jung were apt to assign meaning to the symbols and elements that occurred in dreams. Many who have followed them have done the same. I believe this is too limiting. It is essential to remember that the meaning of an object may differ dramatically from one individual to another. A train in a dream may mean excitement and travel to someone who is going on a journey, may indicate to another that an unwelcome visitor is coming to call, and something sexual to still another.

Of course, some dreams are just what they appear to be. If you dream that you are involved sexually with someone you are attracted to, we have an obvious meaning. But most dreams are not that obvious. In fact, they usually disguise, distort, and conceal their meanings. Dream analysis is an attempt to move beyond the disguises and distortions.

There are several ways to reach the meaning of the disguised, or symbolic, dreams. First, try to get at the feeling you had as you dreamed. Were you sad, happy, frightened, guilty? The emotions that accompanied the dream and those that follow as you examine it are a clue to what the dream is telling you.

A dream may activate old feelings, providing a springboard for further imaginary situations. For example, in a dream you may see someone showing a great deal of anger toward you. This may recall a time in the past when your father expressed anger toward you. You can then use imagery to confront your father, deal with his anger, and deal with archaic feelings you are still responding to.

Sometimes I ask for a title to a dream. This is often useful for focusing on the most important element of the dream. Then I ask for the most opposite title. This may clarify the meaning, and sometimes serves to refine the feelings connected with the dream.

The Most-or-Least technique may be brought into play to explore an element of the dream, or even the title of the dream. For example, one person titled her dream, "The Train." I then asked her to tell me the most unlikely person to be on the train. She answered, "My father." He played no part at all in the dream. She reflected that she "... never did anything with him as a youngster." In this light, the dream began to make sense to her, and she connected it to her present behavior with her boyfriend, Frank. Also, the phrase "to please" appeared in her dream several times. On this basis, I inquired who was the most difficult person for her to please, and who was the easiest person to please? At this point she experienced a flash of anger at Frank for the difficulties he always set up to prevent being pleased by anything she did. Her anger gave her the insight needed to become aware of how she was being defined by him and allowed her to decide to take action.

Her dream involved a train ride in the course of which she was trying to please Frank. He did not seem to respond to her; he did not seem to know how to handle himself in the social situation of the dining car, etc. She was frustrated as she tried to buttress his self-confidence and overlook his lack of sophistication. I asked her to imagine two different trains, using Dual Imagery. She gave this response:

1. Very streamlined—sleek, sophisticated
2. Big, chuggy—old-fashioned like my mother

She then volunteered that she was the sleek train, and Frank was the unsophisticated, big, chuggy train. She felt about him just as she had always felt about her mother. The meaning of this did not escape her, nor did Frank escape her feelings of anger.

Many dreams indicate some internal conflict. Try to recognize the elements in opposition and then contrast those elements. If your dream involves a fight with someone, that is a clear indication of a conflict. If, however, the representation is more subtle, you may have to do some additional imagery to find the source of the conflict.

Suppose you dreamed of an unusual bird that you had never seen before. Get the image of that bird in your mind and then give it an adjective. Now imagine the most opposite image to that unusual bird. What are the outstanding differences between these two images? When you focus on the differences, you can usually find meaning and some form of interpretation. You can do this for any puzzling image in a dream.

You may find it helpful to check out where the dream took place—the physical location or setting of the dream itself. Many times one location has greater emotional significance than another. What feelings are associated with that location? How does the location relate to your current life situation?

Certainly, the people you see in your dreams are significant. It is a good idea to imagine the people in the dream and to imagine what they might say to you. Carry on a dialogue with all of them. If there are unidentifiable persons in the dream, I suggest you "guess" their names. The "guessed" names may relate strongly not only to the dream, but also to people in your waking life. Be sure to carry on a dialogue with the people you do not recognize. This can be a source of enormous meaning.

Two things to keep in mind at all times while exploring your dreams are:

1. How you are defining yourself in the dream.
2. How you feel others in the dream are defining you.

In any dream interpretation, it is possible to take any part of a remembered dream and then do image associations for that particular part. Look for patterns emerging from the spontaneous imagery and deduce specific meaning. Imagining that you are each of the various parts of the dream (as the Gestalt therapists are fond of emphasizing) is beyond question a valuable approach.

Many dreams are not about persons. Yet, since dreams are reflections of your inner life, even the nonperson things in a dream must relate back to the dreamer. Let us assume that you dream about a large brown table that has food on it. Here is what you can do:

Imagine you *are* that table and allow the feelings to emerge as you finish the following stems:

I feel ______________________________.
Best adjective to describe me is______________.
I wish ______________________________.
I must ______________________________.
I secretly ___________________________.
I will ______________________________.
Never refer to me as___________________.

When you have finished all the stems, examine your answers and see if you can get some meaning from them. You will probably find a few good clues.

Another approach is to go back to that original table with food on it. Imagine it again. Now try to imagine the most opposite image to the table. If you compare the images, you often gain additional meaning. Now see if you can humanize the images.

By now you are aware that many of the techniques you have learned for dealing with your waking images are just as effective for interpreting your dreams. Use them to make your dreams work for you.

Before we move on to Special Images, I want to mention briefly two other types of images: hypnogogic and hypnopompic. Don't let the names intimidate you. They are just high-class ways of indicating the fleeting images you have just before you fall asleep (hypnogogic) and those you have just before you are fully awake (hypnopompic).

If you can recall them and desire to do so, you can treat them as you would any of your images or dreams. Since they occur in that hazy area between waking and sleeping, they are sure to be significant.

H. Silberer in David Rapoport's book, *Organization and Pathology of Thought*, observed another type of imagery which he called the autosymbolic phenomenon. This refers to the process of converting abstract thoughts into concrete symbolic images. Silberer first experienced this type of imagery when he was resting and comparing the philosophies of Kant and Schopenhauer. Having fixed the Kantian philosophy in his mind, he began to examine Schopenhauer, then discovered he could not recall the first. His effort to remember was suddenly converted to an image of himself asking for information from a secretary who gave him an unfriendly, rejecting look. The image then reminded him of what he had forgotten—the Kantian philosophy. The sudden, vivid image surprised him, as did the appropriateness of the image. On another occasion, while thinking about a rough passage in something he was writing, Silberer imagined himself planing a piece of wood.

Silberer first wrote of this type of imagery in 1909, but once again we have an example of someone noticing a mental process and writing about it only to have it sink into oblivion for decades. Almost half a century passed before R. L. Munroe "rediscovered" the autosymbolic phenomenon and wrote about it in 1955.

The autosymbolic phenomenon must occur in us quite often. It is probably much more common than we realize, but it occurs so quickly and fleetingly that we lose sight of it most of the time. If you watch for it and become aware of your mental imagery, you will probably discover yourself doing the same thing.

A psychologist told me of an instance of imagining an auto accident. He had never had an automobile accident and did not know why the image should suddenly appear to him. Then he recalled that he had changed an appointment with a client whose husband and child had been killed in a tragic auto accident. His concern to remember the changed appointment was converted to the image of the accident. After this incident, he had no further similar images.

We have by no means exhausted the catalogue of images that express our private worlds. You have been introduced, briefly, to Dual Imagery, Self-Imagery, Body Imagery, Sexual Imagery, and Task Imagery, and you have learned some of the ways Psycho-Imagination Therapy uses them to pinpoint conflicts and to solve problems. I have used all successfully in private therapy with patients and in group therapy.

There is, however, an equally vast number of images and imaginary situations which do not fall into any of the above categories, but which are just as fruitful in revealing your unique, private world. I suggest you try some, or all, of them.

To begin:

> Imagine you are lying on your back and looking up; then imagine you are lying on your stomach and looking down.

What did you see, feel, and do? The emotional content is important in this image, as it has been in all the others. Pay particular attention to your feelings as you experience the image. What meaning do you get from this situation? Can you guess what it is telling you? Very often the image you have while lying on your back and looking up relates to your world view at the time. Does the image begin to have more meaning for you? If you were lying on your back on top of a grassy knoll, looking up at a beautiful, expansive sky, feeling the warm breeze on your body, and experiencing a sense of peace and happiness, that is probably an expression of how you are viewing your world at this moment. If you are feeling particularly oppressed or gloomy, your image may be of storm clouds about to burst, or of a very cold, gray, gloomy landscape.

What did you see and feel when you rolled over onto your stomach and looked down? Were you in the same place as when you imagined lying on your back? Or had you been transported through imagery to a different place? You may be on a beach, atop a hill, in bed, on the floor. Although the image will probably not be sexual in content, it very often relates to your sexuality. It may indicate your attitudes about sex: whether you are comfortable with it, fear it, are frustrated by it. It may reveal some repressed sensuality. Occasionally, it will be more specific and deal with a sexual partner and some aspects of the relationship between you.

The next image is unstructured and free flowing.

Imagine walking down a road. Report twenty images you see.

Write down the twenty images. Write an adjective or a feeling for each. Now examine your images carefully. Is there a story or a pattern that ties them together? Are there some similarities and differences that are outstanding? Are they all light and cheerful? Are they all frightening? Which type of image is predominant?

Continue to ask questions of yourself about these images. Are there people in your images? Who are they? Have dialogues with them.

Which image is the most vivid? Which is the least vivid? Which elicits the most feeling? What kind of emotions do you feel?

As you think about these images, you will begin to see what things, persons, and events are uppermost in your mind. You may encounter an unexpected feeling related to one of the images. You may suddenly get a new perspective on an old situation. I feel sure that you will uncover something that will take on a new importance to you.

Let us turn to an entirely different imaginary situation. First let your imagery flow and follow it through. When you have finished, see if you can guess what the image is revealing.

> Imagine a sealed can under water. What do you see in the can? What do you do with it? How do you feel about the can and its contents?

Have you guessed what the image means? This image often leads to unconscious material. The fact that the can is sealed may lead you to image something you have sealed off from awareness. The additional fact that it is under water suggests that it is in the depths of your mind. Think carefully about whatever you find in the can. It may be a clue to something of importance in your life that you have closed off but would like to deal with. If it is an image that presents a conflict or an unproductive strategy, you can use the processes you have learned throughout the book to come to grips with it. If what is in the can is a source of pain, you can confront it, have a dialogue with it, interact with it. Then if you do not like what has been happening in your imagery, you are free to redo the image in a way that is more suitable and satisfying.

Now try the following image and see what it will tell you:

Imagine reaching into a cupboard. What do you find?

Again, let your imagery flow. Check out the feelings associated with the image. Were you happy, guilty, frightened? Did you like what you found in the cupboard?

This image also deals with unconscious material. As with all other images, what you find in the cupboard is something only you can imagine. It is something from your private, inner world. It must be important to you because you are the one who put it in the cupboard, and you are the one who took it out.

Sometimes the contents of the cupboard are directly related to your situation of the moment. One woman reached in and found a steaming hot turkey dinner. She laughed and told me that she had not had time to have dinner before coming to the office.

Another woman reached into the cupboard and found dishes. When she examined them, she realized they were the pattern her mother had used at home many years ago. She was then able to get in touch with her homesickness and recognized a desire to go back and visit her family.

One man reached into the cupboard and felt his hand caught in a mouse trap. He realized that he was often afraid to try new ventures because he feared getting "trapped" or "hurt."

Here is yet another image which may give you some unexpected insights into yourself:

> Imagine a lock attached to something, and then imagine a series of keys. Choose one key to open the lock.

Did you have difficulty finding the right key? What did you find when you opened the lock? To what was the lock attached? Does this image have significance for you?

I find that people often unlock deep feelings, perhaps the most secret feelings they possess. At some point in the sequence of imagery you may need to redo some aspect of it or be urged on. Do continue the image to its conclusion. You will find it worthwhile.

A forty-year-old man, torn between living his own life or living another person's life, leaving him in limbo, reported his response to this image:

> I instantly saw a large, very old-style lock on a large steel door in a steel wall—all of it colored gun-metal. It was dark, but I could see the wall and door. Its surface was very smooth and cold and covered with moisture, like dewdrops. This was all apprehended immediately, and just as quickly I saw in my hand a ring of keys, all of which, save one, were old, rusted, and unused. The exception—which I felt without hesitation, would open the lock—was made of gold and had brilliant rubies and emeralds encrusting it. I put it in the lock and immediately the door opened and I beheld a brilliantly colored world. It contained everything our ordinary world has, but the colors were so intense, I was caught breathless and be-

came afraid. I immediately felt it was the world I could have if I just would reach out and take it. I fearfully ventured out and saw the intense color lessen but remain naturally strong.

I looked back at the door and saw it still against the rear of the wall. I saw that part of this new world that would exist if the door were closed. I knew that if I ever closed it, that I would be forever in this new, delightful world and that I could never, even if I tried, get back to that dark limbolike tomb.

Looking back at "limbo," the dark side of the door, I saw a woman—she may have been my mother, my wife, or as I said at the time, a Brand-X female. My mother beckoned me back into limbo and pointed to another world. She seemed to deny my right to be in my world and imply that either I should live in limbo or her world.

My world was full of intense colors; many things were irridescent and when things, birds, people, etc., moved, they left trails of color behind them for several feet. In my mother's world, the colors were almost of sunset or dawn: reds, yellows, purples, blacks, but not somber. I didn't like it because of the limited range of color. I knew that given a choice, I would prefer limbo to living in her world and that I could reject her world without worrying about her feelings.

My wife also beckoned me in a like manner and while my mother had beckoned me, I have not even gone into limbo or her world, but had seen it from afar and had rejected it. But when my wife beckoned me, I crossed limbo and went into her world which was colored in all colors of pastel. The contours were soft. No mountains, canyons, or places of danger existed in her world.

She seemed to indicate without words that in

order to have her love, not only must I accept her world as valid for her, but that I must live in it wholly, make it my own and renounce my own world. To me, this was merely a soft prison and, if I were to accept it, its lack of surprise and excitement would bore me. Again, I would choose "limbo" to this if forced to. I would prefer to live in my own world.

My world was not exclusive. I visualized a woman in my world. She seemed to be in it but not constrained by it. I did not feel that she had rejected or accepted it as her own vision of life. We simply talked. I didn't withhold my appreciation of her nor she of me. It was very pleasant.

About this time, Joe asked me to close the door back into limbo. Since I had repeatedly indicated that I felt that if I could, it would be closed forever, I felt that all it required was an exercise of will to close the door; but when asked to do this, I felt a great reluctance to do it. I felt that the woman in limbo would be intensely hurt or injured and, at the same time, I felt if I didn't close it, I'd be back in limbo soon myself. Trying very hard, the most I could do was to shut it to the point that just its outline appeared. In order to make it easier, I imagined a vision of me as I might be. I saw beautiful scenes and places, all of these to the point of closing the door.

I then allowed just any scene to come up, and I saw a volcano in violent eruption. But in all these circumstances, the almost invisible outline of the door persisted over them. At this point, however, I realized that even if I ever returned to limbo, I would never close the door and that sooner or later I'd leave limbo for good and live in my own world.

I feel the image shows my perpetual double bind about living. If I live in my world, I'll hurt those with whom I live and if I give into them, I won't be able to live except in some kind of limbo. Living in limbo denies me to them and them to me. I feel it is an expression of anger at not being allowed to be myself which punished the significant other and also myself.

I am now going to suggest a powerful imaginary situation. You will benefit most from it by allowing yourself plenty of time to follow the entire sequence. It is longer than most of the images you have done, so I am going to break it into sections. Read each carefully and do it before moving on to the next part. Take as much time as you need with each before you proceed to the next. Fix the image and the feelings firmly in your mind or, better yet, jot them down or put them on audio tape.

Imagine reaching into a cave. What do you find? How do you feel? What happens?

Now reach farther into the cave. What do you find? How do you feel? What happens?

Now for the third time, reach even farther into the cave. What happens? What do you find? How do you feel?

I have found that this image nearly always produces strong reactions. Some of the most important emotions, thoughts, and experiences in your life will surface. This image probes deep, deep, deeper into your unconscious to bring forth the most pressing problems, the most hidden secrets, or the most innermost essence of yourself.

Be bold! Examine each part of the image to determine what is central to your life and your being. Look for the ways that you undermine yourself; for the things you allow others to do to, or for, you; for your strengths and weaknesses; for your fears, sorrows, anguish, and pleasures.

One woman reached in and felt a bear. She felt some fear, but on instructions she reached in farther and felt his mouth—the menacing teeth, the wet tongue. She was so frightened that her breath was coming rapidly and she broke out in a cold sweat, but she persevered and when I instructed her to reach even farther into the cave, she reached beyond the bear into a safe, warm, gentle place.

She was able to make the connection between the bear and her father, whom she feared. She examined her feelings about him, the anxiety about being "eaten alive" by him, and her need to deal with those feelings. She realized that she had confronted him, through imagery, and had gone past the menace and had moved to a safer place where she could deal with other terrors by facing them and conquering them.

Sometimes people merely reach into the cave, a little farther each time. Others actually enter it, going deeper and deeper inside. In a large percentage of cases, the imagers find fearsome or distasteful images the first two times. Very often by the third entry, they have come to a safer, more tranquil place, thus discovering that when they persist in facing and overcoming their private demons, they uncover hidden strengths and courage.

If you retreated before you completed the image, you were probably terrified by what you found. I urge you to keep trying until you can do the image entirely. Remember, each time you redo it, you will learn something new. You may have to wait days, weeks, or months until you are ready to redo the image, but *it can be done!*

If you found only pleasant, nonthreatening, fairy-tale images, it could mean that you are fairly free of fears and defenses. On the other hand, it more probably means that your defenses are so strong, your strategies are so fixed, or your fears are so magnified, that you will not allow them to be expressed.

Whatever you find in your cave is really a part of you. Trust your images and trust your ability to transform them. Search for the meaning and your reward will be well worth the effort, for you will come to know yourself in a new way and increase your ability to cope with the revealed self and with the world you live in.

Here, now, is a final imaginary situation. Once again I remind you to take your time, let the sequence flow, and pay close attention to the feelings that accompany the images.

> Imagine you are in a room as a baby. Now imagine growing up in three to five minutes.

You probably had a series of pictures of yourself at different ages. They were probably emotionally charged events in your life. Look at those incidents to determine why they were important enough to stay with you. Watch carefully for the strategies you used to maintain your "alien" identity—that which was conferred on you in your formative years.

Did you feel imprisoned, trapped in that room? Did you stay? Did you leave? Did you walk out, or did you have to fight your way out? What does that tell you?

Were the various sequences pleasant or unpleasant? What early traumas did you relive? What joys did you experience? Ask yourself why you recalled those particular scenes and feelings. Try to recapture the responses that led you to be the person you are today.

Here is an example of a five-minute life history:

> . . . Just a baby? I feel all alone as a baby. All alone in a cold room with no blankets and I can scream for blankets, but I don't think anybody cares to hear me or comes to me. I just get a little older, feeling "cold" like that is like I am supposed to be and hanging onto my Teddy Bear for some kind of warmth. And I get a little older and I develop some kind of allergy, like I get hives and I am breaking out in a rash and then they figure I am allergic to the Teddy Bear, so they take that away from me and they don't let me have any stuffed toys. That really happened too. And then when I start getting old enough to wear dresses, they will take me out of the room and dress me up and then take me for a ride, both my father and my mother. And they take me out in the sunlight and then take me places and then I get sick, or my mother says I'm sick, so we have to go home. They take me into the bathroom and give me an enema and they put me back in my room, and I hear them begin their fighting and I feel they are fighting about me.
>
> And then I get old enough to go to school and they take me to the school and my father walks with me to school and I feel very, very alone at

school. I don't seem to have anybody over to play with me or go anyplace to play with anybody else, like they expect me to be good alone in my room.

... And then after I start getting old enough to go to school, I can hear them tell me that I have to do good in school and I have to have a lot of friends in school. My mother says to me, "Why don't you have any friends and why aren't you making a lot of friends?" She and my father are fighting all the time over me and then when I start having to date with boys, when I am about thirteen, and I don't have any boyfriends and then she starts pushing me at boys. She starts getting involved in things that I'll be involved in boys, like clubs and pushing me to go to parties and asking me questions when I go to the parties like, Do the boys like me? And am I pretty next to the other children? Do the boys want to kiss me?

And then my father goes away and I don't remember my father now and he is out of the house. There is just her and me. When I get old enough to go to high school, the same stuff. "Why aren't you doing this? Why aren't you doing that?" And she looks so involved in what I am doing or what I am supposed to be doing.

... If she would have just let me grow up inside that room until ... I feel like I am getting so tall that I am hitting my head on the ceiling, but I don't have any of my things in the room and I don't even have my clothes in the room. It's like I just live in there, but I don't have anything in there and I feel like I am too big for that room and I am just too big to even sit in a chair in that room. My head keeps growing out through the ceiling, like I have to pull myself in and just huddle, sit in there to be big enough for it. The more I get to be my age now, I would be huge in that room—growing, growing huge.

After finishing with your five-minute life history, you can ask yourself, "What are the two most significant events in my life?" You may find the point when a neurotic resolution was tightened or a time when you were able to broach some healthy conflict resolution. I have heard in response to that question, "When I first went to college away from home." "When I was in the army and I realized that sex was an open subject and that I didn't have to be guilty about it." "The time I went home to my mother's outstretched arms after I flunked out of medical school." Or, "At the age of ten when my father died and I had to be an adult."

We have barely scratched the surface of the many imaginary situations that I have used over the past twelve years. But you now have a working knowledge of the kinds of images and what they can tell you. If you have been doing the imagery as you read through the book, you can continue to work with images and dreams whenever they come to your awareness.

Reread your images from time to time. If you have put them on audio tape, replay them. New insights will come with a change in perspective and with a change in life situations. People who have been doing imagery for many years, and have done certain ones repeatedly, are frequently surprised to see the changes that occur when they redo a familiar image.

I want to repeat once again that your imagery can have a tremendous impact upon your life and upon those persons you are dealing with. It can arouse emotions; it can affect your health; it can produce changes in your environment—both physical and social. It seems only right and proper that you use such an extraordinarily potent part of your mental activity.

You live in a world of images. Be aware of them. Explore them to know and understand their nature. Allow your images to reveal yourself to yourself. Let them span time and relate past objects and experiences to present objects and experiences. Use your imagery as a bridge from past to present so that you can learn to tolerate what you must and can change what you must for a more satisfactory future.

Let imagery free your creativity. As you learn to be more creative in your imagery, you can develop deeper understanding of your feelings and your life. Utilizing your imagery expands your horizons. You are starting an endless process of fulfilling your potential.

Finally, as you continue to use your imagery, you will probably feel a revival of curiosity. You may become more adventuresome and more exploratory. In an age of alienation this is a worthy goal.

Appendix

WARM-UP EXERCISES

Here are a few warm-up exercises for people who doubt their ability to do imagery. There are some to stimulate each of the five senses just to prove to you that you not only have the ability to have visual images, but you can also experience auditory, olfactory, gustatory, and tactile imagery.

Relax, close your eyes, and let the imagery flow.

VISUAL

1. Ocean waves breaking on the shore
2. City lights at night seen from a hilltop
3. A tree
4. The freeway at rush hour
5. Stars on a clear winter night
6. The "mushroom" cloud from an atomic-bomb blast

7. The sun as it sinks below the horizon
8. A football stadium
9. A flash of lightning
10. Your own name as you write it

AUDITORY

1. Loud laughter
2. The ring of a telephone
3. Church bells ringing
4. An alarm clock going off
5. A dog barking
6. The clinking of glasses
7. Rain on the roof
8. The slam of a door
9. The clapping of hands in applause
10. A high wind

OLFACTORY

1. Cooking fish
2. Perfume
3. Something burning
4. Gasoline
5. Cigar smoke
6. Roses
7. Decaying garbage
8. Fresh paint
9. Onions
10. Ammonia

GUSTATORY

1. Chocolate
2. Salt

3. Sugar
4. Lemon
5. Ice cream
6. Pepper
7. Watermelon
8. Candy
9. Toothpaste
10. Peanut butter

TACTILE

1. Feeling the touch of fur
2. The prick of a pin
3. The touch of a baby's cheek
4. A toothache
5. The touch of a man's whiskers
6. A very tight shoe
7. Rubbing grease between two fingers
8. Touching something hot
9. A stomach-ache
10. Rubbing your finger over sandpaper

Bibliography

CHAPTER I

Ashton-Warner, Sylvia. *Spearpoint.* New York: Alfred A. Knopf, 1972.

Downs, Roger M. and Stea, David. *Image and Environment.* Chicago: Aldine Publishing Co., 1973.

Irving, Washington. "The Stout Gentleman." *In Selected Writings of Washington Irving.* New York: Modern Library, 1945.

Jellinek, Augusta. Spontaneous Imagery: A New Psychotherapeutic Approach. In *American Journal of Psychotherapy*, Vol. 3, No. 3, July 1949.

Kafka, Franz. "The Metamorphosis." In Nahum N. Glatzer (ed.), *The Complete Stories.* New York: Schocken Books, 1971.

Klinger, Eric. *Structure and Functions of Fantasy.* New York: Wiley Interscience, 1971.

Kris, Ernest. *Psychoanalytic Explorations in Art.* London: George Allen and Unwin, Ltd., 1953.

Lippmann, Walter. *A Preface to Politics.* New York: The Macmillan Company, 1928.
Nelson, Portia. *There's a Hole in My Sidewalk.* New York: Popular Library, 1977.
Shorr, Joseph E. *Psycho-Imagination Therapy.* New York: Intercontinental Medical Book Corporation, 1972.
Shorr, Joseph E. *Psychotherapy Through Imagery.* New York: Intercontinental Medical Book Corporation, 1974.
Skorokhodova, O. I. How I Perceive and Picture the World Around Me. In *A Handbook of Contemporary Soviet Psychology*. Michael Cole and Irving Maltzman (eds.), New York: Basic Books, 1969.
Witkin, H. S. "Orientation in Space." In *Research Reviews.* Office of Naval Research, December 1949.

CHAPTER II

Bettelheim, Bruno. "The Uses of Enchantment." In *American Psychological Association Monitor*, Vol. 7, No. 2, February 1976.
Breuer, Josef, and Freud, Sigmund. *Studies in Hysteria.* A.A. Brill (trans.), Boston: Beacon Press, 1950.
Ellenberger, Henri F. *The Discovery of the Unconscious.* New York: Basic Books, 1970.
Ferenczi, Sándor. *The Theory and Technique of Psychoanalysis.* New York: Basic Books, 1952.
Gary, Romain. *The Roots of Heaven.* New York: Simon and Schuster, 1958.
Laing, R.D. *The Self and Others.* Chicago: Quadrangle Books, 1960.
May, Rollo. *Existence.* New York: Basic Books, 1958.
Singer, Jerome L. "Imagery and Daydream Techniques Employed in Psychotherapy: Some Practical and Theoretical Implications." In C. Spielberger (ed.), *Current Topics in Clinical and Community*

Psychology, New York; Academic Press, 1971, Vol. 3.

Shorr, Joseph E. "The Existential Question and the Imaginary Situation as Therapy." In *Existential Psychiatry*, 6:24:443–462, Winter 1967.

Weisskopf-Joelson, Edith. "Experimental Studies of Meaning Through Integration." In *Patterns of Integration from Biochemical to Behavioral Process.* Annals of the New York Academy of Sciences, Vol. 193, 260–72.

CHAPTER III

Bakan, David. "Hypnotizability, Laterality of Eye Movements and Brain Asymmetry." In *Perceptual and Motor Skills.* 1969.

Black, Johnny S. *Paper Doll.* Edward B. Marks Music Corp., 1925.

Blau, Theodore. *The Sinister Child.* Paper presented at American Psychological Association Convention, New Orleans, 1974.

Gombrich, E.H. *Art and Illusion.* Princeton: Princeton University Press, 1960.

Horney, Karen. *Neurosis and Human Growth.* New York: W.W. Norton, 1950.

London, Jack. *The Star Rover.* New York: The Macmillan Company, 1963.

News of the World. London: September 1, 1970.

Reich, Wilhelm. *Character Analysis.* 3rd ed., New York: Orgone Institute Press, 1949.

Shorr, Joseph E. "Dual Imagery." In *Psychotherapy: Theory, Research and Practice*, Vol. 13, No. 2, Fall 1976.

Shorr, Joseph E. Psychotherapy Through Imagery, I, demonstrates uses of "dual imagery". The Center for Cassette Studies, Inc., 8110 Webb Ave. North Hollywood, CA 91605. No. 36640.

Stevenson, Robert Louis. "The Strange Case of Doctor Jekyll and Mr. Hyde." In *The Complete Short Stories of Robert Louis Stevenson*, Charles Neilder (ed.), Garden City: Doubleday & Co., Inc., 1969.

CHAPTER IV

Horney, Karen. *Neurosis and Human Growth*, New York: W.W. Norton, 1950.

Klein, George S. "Peremptory Ideation Structure and Force in Motivated Ideas." In Richard Jessor and Seymour Fashback (eds.) *Cognition, Personality, and Clinical Psychology*. San Francisco: Jossey-Bass, 1967.

Lewis, William C. *Why People Change*. New York: Holt, Rinehart and Winston Co., 1972.

Moravia, Alberto. *A Ghost at Noon*. London: Penguin Books, Ltd., 1955.

Rank, Otto. *Will Therapy*. New York: Alfred A. Knopf, 1936.

Sartre, Jean-Paul. *The Words*. Greenwich: Fawcett Premier Books, 1964.

Sullivan, Harry Stack. *The Interpersonal Theory of Psychiatry*. New York: W.W. Norton, 1953.

Wheelis, Alan. *The Seeker*. New York: Random House, 1960.

CHAPTER V

Auden, W.H. Prologue. "The Birth of Architecture." In *About the House*. New York: Random House, 1965.

Fisher, Seymour. *Body Experience in Fantasy and Behavior*. New York: Appleton, Century, Crofts, 1970.

Seidenberg, R. "Who Owns the Body?" In *Existential Psychiatry*, Summer-Fall 1969, (93–105).

Shorr, Joseph E. "In What Part of Your Body Does Your Mother Reside?" In *Psychotherapy: Theory, Research and Practice*, 10:2:31–34, Summer, 1973.

Shorr, Joseph E. "Body Focusing" *Psychotherapy Through Imagery II.* Center for Cassette Studies, Inc., 8110 Webb Ave. North Hollywood, CA. No. 36641.

Tolstoy, Leo. *Childhood, Boyhood and Youth.* London: Penguin Books, Ltd., 1967.

CHAPTER VI

Benjamin, Harry and R.E.L. Masters. *Prostitution and Morality: A Definitive Report on the Prostitute in Contemporary Society and an Analysis of the Causes and Effects of the Suppression of Prostitution.* New York: Julian Press, 1964.

Frankl, Victor. *Man's Search for Meaning.* Boston: Beacon Press, 1966.

Jones, Ernest. "Jealousy". In *Papers on Psychoanalysis.* London: Balliere, Tindall and Cox, Ltd., 1937.

Kronhausen, Drs. Phyllis and Eberhard. *Erotic Fantasies.* New York: Grove Press, Inc., 1969.

Laing, R.D. *The Self and Others.* Chicago: Quadrangle Books, 1962.

Singer, Jerome L. and Hariton, Barbara. "Women's Fantasies During Sexual Intercourse: Normative and Theoretical Implications." In *Journal of Consulting and Clinical Psychology*, 42 (3) 313–22, 1974.

Shorr, Joseph E. *Sexual Imagery.* The Center for Cassette Studies, Inc., 8110 Webb Ave., North Hollywood, CA 91605. No. 39499.

Tolstoy, Leo. *Kreutzer Sonata.* New York: Thomas Crowell Co., 1899.

CHAPTER VII

Fromm, Erich. "Remarks on the Problem of Free Association." In *Psychiatric Research Reports 2*, American Psychiatric Association, 1955.

Gorman, James. "Mind and the Athlete." In *The Sciences*, Vol. 15, No. 2, March 1975.

James, William. *Principles of Psychology*. New York: Henry Holt and Company, 1890.
Murphy, Gardner. *Personality, a Biosocial Approach to Origins and Structure*. New York: Harper and Row, 1947.
Shorr, Joseph E. "Task Imagery as Therapy." In *Psychotherapy: Theory, Research and Practice*. Vol. 12, No. 2, Summer 1975.
Shorr, Joseph E. "Task Imagery." *Psychotherapy Through Imagery II*. The Center for Cassette Studies, Inc., 8110 Webb Ave. North Hollywood, CA 91605. No. 36641.

CHAPTER VIII

Barron, Frank. *Creativity and Personal Freedom*. New York: D. Van Nostrand, 1968.
Ellenberger, Henri F. *The Discovery of the Unconscious*. New York: Basic Books, 1970.
Freud, Sigmund. *The Interpretation of Dreams*. A. A. Brill (trans.) New York: Modern Library, 1950.
Munroe, R.L. *Schools of Psychoanalytic Thought*. New York: Dryden Press, 1955.
Silberer, H. "On Symbol Formation." In David Rapoport, *On Organization and Pathology of Thought*. New York: Columbia University Press, 1951.
Shorr, Joseph E. "Clinical Use of Categories of Therapeutic Imagery." In J.L. Singer and K. Pope (eds.), *The Power of Human Imagination*. New York: Plenum Publishing Co. (in press).
Shorr, Joseph E. *Psycho-Imagination Therapy*, Center for Cassette Studies, Inc., 8110 Webb Ave. North Hollywood, CA 91605. No. 33818.
Varendonck, J. *The Psychology of Daydreams*. New York: The Macmillan Company, 1921.

Updated Bibliography

Connella, Jack. The uses of self-image imagery in psychotherapy. In J. Shorr, J. Connella, P. Robin, G. Sobel-Whittington (Eds.), *Imagery,* Vol. III. New York: Plenum Press, (in press).

Robin, Pennee. Theory and application of psycho-imagination therapy. In J. Shorr, G. Sobel, P. Robin, and J. Connella (Eds.), *Imagery: its many dimensions and applications,* Vol. I. New York: Plenum Press, 1980.

Robin, Pennee. Integration of sullivanian theory and the use of imagery in couples therapy. In J. Shorr, J. Connella, P. Robin, G. Sobel-Whittington (Eds.), *Imagery,* Vol. III. New York: Plenum Press (in press).

Shorr, Joseph E. Imagery as a projective device. In B. Virshup (Ed.), Imagery Bulletin. Los Angeles: American Association for the Study of Mental Imagery, Vol. I, No. 2, July, 1978.

Shorr, Joseph E. Imagery as a method of self-observation in therapy. In B. Virshop (Ed.) Imagery Bulletin. Los Angeles: American Association for the Study of Mental Imagery, Vol. II, No. 2, May, 1979.

Shorr, Joseph E. How the mind organizes and finds meaning in imagery. In J. Shorr, G. Sobel, P. Robin, and J. Connella (Eds.), *Imagery: its many dimensions and applications.* New York: Plenum Press, 1980.

Shorr, Joseph E. An overview of psycho-imagination therapy. In R. Corsini (Ed.), *Innovative psychotherapies.* New York: Wylie Interscience, 1981.

Shorr, Joseph E. The psychologist's imagination and sexual imagery. In E. Klinger (Ed.), *Imagery: concepts, results and applications*. New York: Plenum Press, 1981.

Shorr, Joseph E. Psycho-imagination therapy's approach to body imagery. In J. Shorr, J. Connella, P. Robin, G. Sobel-Whittington (Eds.), *Imagery,* Vol. III. New York: Plenum Press, (in press).

Sobel, Gail. A group study using the group shorr imagery test as the tool of outcome therapy. In J. Shorr, G. Sobel, P. Robin, J. Connella (Eds.), *Imagery: its many dimensions and applications.* New York: Plenum Press, 1980.

Tansey, David. Use of the shorr imagery test with a population of violent offenders. In J. Shorr, G. Sobel, P. Robin, J. Connella (Eds.), *Imagery: its many dimensions and applications*, Vol. I. New York: Plenum Press, 1980.

Tansey, David. Correlation of the shorr imagery test and the imaginal processes inventory. In J. Shorr, J. Connella, P. Robin, G. Sobel-Whittington (Eds.), *Imagery,* Vol. III. New York: Plenum Press (in press).

Tansey, David. Psycho-imagination sand play. The professional psychologist; March–April 1983, Volume 7, No. 2.